History Class Revisited

Learn new approaches to teaching history in middle school so students are more engaged in the big ideas and eager to examine the world around them. Co-published by Routledge and MiddleWeb, this practical guide will help you consider the unique needs of middle schoolers, who are in the midst of many social and emotional changes and need to see why the study of history matters to their own lives. Author Jody Passanisi shares helpful strategies and activities to make your social studies class a place where students can relate to the material, connect past history to present events, collaborate with others, think critically about important issues, and take ownership of their learning. Topics include:

- ◆ Reading and analyzing primary and secondary sources for deeper comprehension of historical issues
- ◆ Developing a written argument and defending it with supporting details and cited sources
- ◆ Examining the social context of a historical event and tracing the historical underpinnings of present-day issues
- ◆ Using field trips, games, and project-based learning to make learning history a fun and interactive experience
- ◆ Assessing your students' progress using self-reflection, projects, essays, and presentations

The appendices offer resources for each of the topics covered in the book, as well as reproducible Blackline Masters of the charts and diagrams, which can be photocopied or downloaded from our website (www.routledge.com/9781138639713) for classroom use.

Jody Passanisi is an eighth-grade U.S. history teacher at an independent school in the Los Angeles area and an adjunct instructor at Mount St. Mary's University.

Other Eye On Education Books, Available from Routledge

(www.routledge.com/eyeoneducation)

The Genius Hour Guidebook:
Fostering Passion, Wonder, and Inquiry in the Classroom
Denise Krebs and Gallit Zvi

STEM by Design:
Strategies and Activities for Grades 4–8
Anne Jolly

The Classes They Remember:
Using Role-Plays to Bring Social Studies and English to Life
David Sherrin

Judging for Themselves:
Using Mock Trials to Bring Social Studies and English to Life
David Sherrin

Common Core in the Content Areas:
Balancing Content and Literacy
Jessica Bennett

DIY Project Based Learning for ELA and History
Heather Wolpert-Gawron

DIY Project Based Learning for Math and Science
Heather Wolpert-Gawron

Writing Behind Every Door:
Teaching Common Core Writing in the Content Areas
Heather Wolpert-Gawron

History Class Revisited

Tools and Projects to Engage Middle School Students in Social Studies

Jody Passanisi

NEW YORK AND LONDON

First published 2016
by Routledge
711 Third Avenue, New York, NY 10017

and by Routledge
2 Park Square, Milton Park, Abingdon, Oxon, OX14 4RN

Routledge is an imprint of the Taylor & Francis Group, an informa business

Library of Congress Cataloging-in-Publication Data
Names: Passanisi, Jody, author.
Title: History class revisited : tools and projects to engage middle school
    students in social studies / by Jody Passanisi.
Description: New York : Routledge, 2016. | Includes bibliographical
    references.
Identifiers: LCCN 2015042824 | ISBN 9781138639706 (hardback) |
    ISBN 9781138639713 (pbk.) | ISBN 9781315637037 (ebook)
Subjects: LCSH: United States—History—Study and teaching (Middle school)
Classification: LCC E175.8 .P37 2016 | DDC 973.071/2—dc23
LC record available at http://lccn.loc.gov/2015042824

ISBN: 978-1-138-63970-6 (hbk)
ISBN: 978-1-138-63971-3 (pbk)
ISBN: 978-1-315-63703-7 (ebk)

Typeset in Palatino
by Apex CoVantage, LLC

To Sebastian:
You made middle school a bit more bearable

Contents

About the Author

Jody Passanisi is a middle-school history teacher in Los Angeles, where she works at an independent school. She has an MA in Religious Studies from the Graduate Theological Union, and an MS in Education from Mount St. Mary's University.

In addition to her work in the classroom, Jody is an adjunct instructor at Mount St. Mary's University in Los Angeles where she works with in-service and pre-service teachers on developing units based on *Understanding by Design* and current social studies methods. She has also worked as a clinical educator for DeLeT's induction program, mentoring teachers through their first years in the classroom.

Jody is a vocal advocate for purposefully incorporating twenty-first century tools and skills into the classroom, and her writing has been featured at *Education Week Teacher*, *Scientific American* and *SmartBrief*. Alongside her colleagues Aaron Brock and Shara Peters, Jody has written about teaching history in the middle grades at MiddleWeb's *Future of History* blog (http://www.middleweb.com/category/futureofhistory/). You can find her on Twitter @21centuryteachr and at 21centuryteachr.wordpress.com.

Jody lives in Los Angeles with her husband and three children.

Acknowledgments

It wouldn't be hyperbolic to say that this book wouldn't exist without my colleagues and collaborators Shara Peters and Aaron Brock. Aaron's ideas about literacy, writing, and his general knowledge of history have always been instrumental when we've planned together. Shara, my writing partner and teaching partner, everything we've done has been better as a team. Your unflagging positivity, creativity, and desire to reflect and improve is something I try to emulate. Our collaboration is reflected throughout this book.

Thank you to mentors and colleagues and all those who have supported and guided me, present and past: Joanne, Lara, Betty, Paula, Larry, and Marc. And to all of my colleagues in both elementary and middle school, I am so lucky to work with you all; you inspire me daily. To Debra, thank you; without you (and Upton Sinclair) I wouldn't even *be* a middle school teacher.

To my mentors at DeLeT, Michael, Luisa, Michelle, Bonnie, Marilyn, Eileen, and Rivka: Thank you for providing the foundation for my career and keeping me in the loop all these years later. And thank you to Julie at Mount St. Mary's University for trusting me to teach social studies to teachers.

To my husband, Sebastian, I wouldn't have thought I could write a book without your encouragement. And I have always appreciated the way you've pushed me to explain myself better in my writing. To our children Levi, Ezra, and Saul you've taught me a lot about early childhood. I can't wait till you guys are in middle school—then I'll know what to do.

Thank you to all of my parents: my mother who never let me feel like I couldn't accomplish anything I wanted to and to my father whose own creativity and success have driven me to try to be successful. To Celeste, who has helped me my whole life, and to Liz, Dennis, Suzann, and Dominic— thank you for all your help and support.

And to my family near and far and friends like family near and far: Becca, Cezanne, Michael, Maura, Isaac, Mary, Laura, Mike, Syndie, Randie, Jamie, and Danit—thank you so much for everything. And to Jenny, your friendship in middle school was paramount.

To John Norton and Susan Curtis and MiddleWeb, your edits, suggestions, and big picture mindset about education have been so helpful to me over these past few years writing for MiddleWeb and for this book.

Thank you to Lauren Davis at Routledge; your ideas, critique, support, and encouragement have been invaluable in this process. And my great appreciation to Emma Håkonsen, Marlena Sullivan, and everyone at Routledge who worked to make this book happen.

I am so appreciative to all of the resources out there for bettering education and re-imaging how the learning can be. Thanks to the Buck Institute and Dr. Gary Stager—together, your work on Project-based Learning has energized my classroom. Thank you to Common Sense Media and Social Studies School Service for the resources you provide for educators. And thank you to all of the other amazing places and people out there for teachers to learn from.

To all my students, present, former, and future; it is for you to decide how we can reach you; thank you for learning with me over these years. It is for you that teachers teach; it's been a pleasure watching you grow up over all these years.

1

Introduction: Teaching Middle School History

It's Not Quite Elementary School . . . It's Not Quite High School

"You teach middle school? Wow. That must be . . . something. That's a difficult age, right?"

That's the reaction I get almost every time I tell people I teach middle school. Why?

Middle schoolers are an interesting breed. Most of them—even those who are *not* struggling because of external stressors—are internally stressed. These 11- to 14-year-olds are in what is termed a liminal stage: They are not quite kids, but certainly not quite adults, or young adults even. They aren't in elementary school anymore, but they aren't ready for high school. They experience changes in their bodies, their brains, their social expectations, and their academics. Their parents and friends react differently to them than they used to, and middle schoolers react differently to their parents and friends. In short, middle school students are in flux and are often struggling to find their footing socially, emotionally, and academically.

So why the strong reaction when I tell people I am a middle school teacher? Often it has less to do with the person's experience of middle school kids in the *present* than their perceptions of their own past, their *own* experience of being a middle schooler and navigating the world with other young adolescents.

Because of all these changes, all this flux, middle school students are often focused on their social and emotional lives more than they are on their academic selves. This book will address the tension between the developmentally appropriate egocentrism of adolescents and the concepts essential to social studies, which call on us to look beyond ourselves to the stories of communities and the history of societies. My goal is to provide strategies that teachers can use to help students make the study of history a part of their social and emotional growth, as students connect with the content through the acquisition of skills, collaboration with others, critical thinking, and increased independence.

The Middle School Brain and the Middle Schooler's Life

The behavioral shifts that occur in the middle years aren't just anecdotal. Middle school students are in the midst of neurological changes: At this age, students' brains are undoing approximately 20 percent of previously forged synaptic connections; they may or may not have access to information and concepts once stored. Additionally, their neocortex hasn't yet fully developed. They aren't going to be experts at the executive functioning tasks that school expects of them: organization, punctuality, and planning (Vawter, 2010).

Also, the hormone-heavy limbic system is working overtime at this age. This is the part of the brain that drives emotions and feelings, and to make matters even more interesting, the prefrontal cortex hasn't fully developed to help the students *handle* those feelings and emotions in a logical way (Giedd, 2015). Neurologically, this is why middle school students are what they are: often impulsive, difficult to predict, and moody. It's no wonder that when they are all jumbled up together in school, there is challenge and conflict. It's no wonder that when students are in the classroom, they are often focused on things other than academic learning. Their brains are pre-wired to put relationships and emotions first, and school isn't always designed well to cope with that inevitable consequence of growing up.

Pedagogical Assumptions about History Class

Perhaps the emotions and relationship *sturm und drang* are the reasons that people often have a negative reaction when looking back at their middle school years. And then there's history and social studies. How does that fit into the middle school experience?

When I started teaching a social studies methods course last year, I was surprised at how many of my students recalled negative experiences in their own social studies classes. There were a few reasons for this: One theme that came up multiple times was that the college students, many of whom were Latinas, didn't feel like the history they learned was about "them" at all. This reaction is valid and relevant, and never more so than when we are teaching middle school students. If students don't feel like the history being studied has something to do with their own experience of the world—if their own cultural background is not represented in the content—then they can feel marginalized.

> If students don't feel like the history being studied has something to do with their own experience of the world—if their own cultural background is not represented in the content—then they can feel marginalized.

Another theme among the college students—the most common, in fact— was that history was "boring" in middle school. They remembered history class as being the class where students read the book and then answered the questions to prepare for a test. It was upsetting (as a passionate history teacher) to hear this, but also not surprising: Wasn't my own history class experience pretty similar?

So what do we make of all this? For middle school students, who are focused primarily on their own relationships, history class needs to be structured in such a way that they *can* connect to the content, both personally and educationally.

To make content relevant, we need to give middle school students good answers to the ever-present question: "How does this apply to me?" As they make connections to their own experiences and to the world they see around them, they begin to find relevance in social studies. By examining the world of the past and the world of *now* in the context of their own identities, they can discover what needs changing and imagine themselves as positive agents of that change.

> By examining the world of the past and the world of *now* in the context of their own identities, they can discover what needs changing and imagine themselves as positive agents of that change.

This developmental rationale for making purposeful connections between the stuff of history and the lives of middle school students is only further reinforced by the current pedagogical and technological shifts that are driving changes in the ways we teach history. History class must be different now than it used to be; pedagogically, history class has been, well, *historically* focused on memorization and fact retrieval. With the advent of the Internet, students have access to those facts (if their teacher allows it) and can look up any information they may need.

This is not to say that this access has made history class irrelevant. Far from it, in fact. The wealth of information now available makes it possible to elevate the social studies/history class to a new level. What's more, as the Common Core's focus on critical reading and writing suggests, students in history class need to master higher level skills to be able to understand, discern, contextualize, and evaluate what they find and read online.

Ready access to historical content should lead teachers to spend less time on memorization during class and to have students spend more time on historiography and other rigorous concepts. Students can delve more deeply into and learn to analyze primary and secondary sources. Students can hone their reading and writing skills for history-specific work. And they can learn how to make connections from the past to the present through historical analysis.

These advances in technology, access to information, and brain research raise the question: What *should* history class look like for our current crop of middle school students? How do we make social studies class personal, relevant, contextual, and pedagogically progressive? How do we get young adolescents excited about history?

The Twenty-First Century Middle School History Teacher

In "Middle School," an episode of NPR's *This American Life*, former teacher Alex Blumberg, who taught middle school science for four years, reflects on his experience:

> I don't know if they learned anything. They are so consumed with learning all these other lessons about where they fit in, in the social order, and how their bodies are now working. . . . I basically came away thinking you're sort of wasting your time trying to teach middle school students anything ("Episode 449: Middle School," *This American Life*, 2011).

Blumberg may sound somewhat over the top (he left teaching to become a radio producer), but those of us who currently do it would certainly agree: It *is* a challenge to be a middle school teacher. Expectations are different from that of an elementary or high school teacher. The stereotypical idea of a teacher in the elementary grades is that of a nurturer, someone who takes care of the emotional needs of the student all day. The archetype of a high school teacher, while also invested in each student, is thought to be tougher, more serious, moving students from adolescence to adulthood and focusing on cultivating each student's academic prowess.

So what's the stereotype of a middle school teacher? Harried or frazzled perhaps, also tough, also nurturing. There really *isn't* a stereotype, but it definitely helps to be flexible and resilient. As Alex Blumberg so candidly shares, sometimes it feels like nothing's getting through. Many long-time middle school teachers might add that other times, you feel like you wouldn't want to be anywhere else than with these wild and crazy middle school kids.

Every middle school teacher needs to be knowledgeable about pedagogy, about history, about human development, and about current trends. We also need to be attentive listeners, "readers of the room," and innovators. At this age, students (and sometimes parents) expect *everything* from a teacher. As they move through early adolescence, they anticipate that their teacher will still be nurturing, will still help them navigate social and emotional challenges that crop up during the day, but will also let them ride without training wheels and show respect for their newfound autonomy. It's certainly as much of a balancing act for the teacher as it is for the student. Well, almost.

Being a middle school *history* teacher means confronting some of the harder truths about history that haven't previously been developmentally appropriate to share with students. For example, students in elementary school are often told Rosa Parks was tired and that's why she wouldn't give up her seat and move to the back of the bus. In middle school, students should be told that Rosa Parks's act was intentional, planned, and part of a larger movement intended to bring about social and legal changes. (Actually, I would argue that students should be told this particular truth in the earlier grades as well. It's never too soon for students to learn about agency and social activism.)

Middle school students will have hard questions about slavery, about the kind of person Lincoln was, about the Holocaust, and about how women have been treated historically. Middle school is the time to

> A middle-level educator looking to help students make connections should be willing to delve deeply into difficult historical subjects ... to help students understand how the world of yesterday became the world of today, and what that might mean for the world of tomorrow.

allow students to discover some of the difficulties of our current world and how these things are rooted in historical context. A middle-level educator looking to help students make connections should be willing to delve deeply into difficult historical subjects—such as prejudice, slavery, and genocide—to help students understand how the world of yesterday became the world of today, and what that might mean for the world of tomorrow.

How Do We Reach Middle Schoolers in History Class?

Specifically, how do we reach and teach middle schoolers in history class? The answer isn't simple. I have not found that one particular pedagogical approach always works with students of this age. From my experience, these students need a combination of approaches, including student-centered pedagogical strategies that help them stretch themselves and feel ownership over concepts and material; interesting and relevant content that connects to their own understandings of the world and that can help them expand that understanding; and academic structures that help them feel safe when so much else in their lives is difficult to predict.

This book walks through some of the strategies, projects, and experiences I have had with students in my eighth-grade classroom and explains how you might try similar ideas. While many of the projects are particular to eighth-grade California content standards (I teach in the Los Angeles area), I try to make the concepts broad enough so that whatever the content, the pedagogical approach can be adjusted to fit. I also provide examples that relate to both sixth- and seventh-grade content. While I don't always address Common Core State Standards (CCSS) in particular, the main CCSS themes are embedded throughout, with emphasis on skills such as critical reading, writing, and thinking.

Having moved some years ago from teaching third grade to teaching middle school, I have to admit that I am biased in favor of this age group, and you will see that throughout the book. I really find this age fascinating. I see it as a unique teaching opportunity, not just a challenge. How can we help create a classroom where our adolescent students are both gaining skills specific to the study of history and *also* learning more about the aspects of themselves that they are so desperately trying to figure out? How can we balance the student-centered, collaborative, creative, project-based aspects of pedagogy with the skills that they will need to succeed in high school? How can we reach them? This book attempts to answer those questions.

References

"Episode 449: Middle School." *This American Life*. National Public Radio. WBEZ. Chicago, IL, 28 Oct. 2011. Web. 8 Aug. 2015. <http://www.this americanlife.org/radio-archives/episode/449/transcript>. Transcript.

Giedd, Jay N. "Risky Teen Behavior Is Driven by an Imbalance in Brain Development." *Scientific American Global RSS*. N.p., June 2015. Web. 27 July 2015.

Vawter, David. "Mining the Middle School Mind." *Education Digest: Essential Readings Condensed For Quick Review* 75.5 (2010): 47–49. ERIC. Web. 8 Aug. 2015.

2

Day to Day

Providing Structure and Routines for a Middle School History Classroom

Middle schoolers may act as if they buck structure—they may roll their eyes the billionth time they have to do a particular routine in a class—but truly structure helps them focus. It helps them ground themselves in the present and differentiate your class from the rest of their work all day.

When I taught third grade, the schedule that I wrote on the board each day was paramount; it was possibly even the focus for some students. If I deviated from the schedule unannounced, my students would be sure to let me know. If something was different, my students would let me know, and if a particular block of time was about to be over, they would let me know. The schedule for them was how they structured their day, how they knew what was going to happen, when, and why. I didn't always have to be specific as to what we were *doing* during math or reading time, but boy did they need to know when math and reading were happening.

Middle schoolers, while possibly more subtle about it, also really want to know what they are doing each day in class.

This can present a problem for me, at times, since many of my lessons are constructivist in nature in that they start with a broad anticipatory set that tries to activate the students' experience without being specific to the content. Sometimes the content is meant to be uncovered and not to be made explicit until later. So I don't write a schedule on the board like I did for my third grade students. Instead, I structure the class so that there are key touch points of routine for the students to latch onto. This helps them feel safe, so that they know (basically) what to expect. For middle school students, there is a fine line between intrigue, novelty, and routine. I try to mix it up content-wise, of course, project-wise, and activity-wise, while keeping skills and other classroom routines, well, routine.

Do Now: When They Walk in the Door

In a middle school, students often travel separately (or with their friends). Like in high school, and unlike in elementary school, there is a straggle-effect. Students aren't always coming in at the same time. Some students will be really early, and though we try to prevent it, some will be late—or, in the best case scenario, they will sneak in right under the wire. I want students to get clear instructions when they come into the room, but it's tough to start the anticipatory set (set induction or beginning activity) if everyone is coming in and starting at different times. Different start times mean that students who work quickly will have downtime on their hands, and students who come in at the last minute won't have enough time to really work on whatever the anticipatory set is that day.

In order to overcome this challenge, I add a "Do Now" to the board. It may be as simple as instructions about materials:

Do Now:
Get out Notes 3: Locke and Jefferson
Set up your notes for QAR

Or, it may ask students to quickly brainstorm something to put either in their notebooks or in a physical communal space, like an IdeaPaint wall or an online communal space like Padlet or a Lino board. For example: On the Idea-Paint wall, write down one thing you are still wondering about Medieval Japan.

These "Do Nows" ground students in predictability, as well as give me a chance to greet the students individually, take care of any ancillary business, give them clear instructions about the supplies they need (computer, notebook, book, etc.), and have them ready to think about the overall themes of the day's topic. In a way, the "Do Now" sets the tone. Students know you have a plan, they know that they will be working, and they know that there will be expectations from the moment they walk in. This can be a class-room management strategy, then, too. So often, middle schoolers opine or

> Middle schoolers are like sharks. If they smell disorganization at the beginning of the class, it is possible you've already lost them.

say with glee (depending on their general attitude toward school) that they "don't do anything" in a certain class. I highly doubt that's true! However, middle schoolers are like sharks. If they smell disorganization at the beginning of the class, it is possible you've already lost them.

When They Have to Take Notes

I often have a mix of students who take notes by hand and students who take notes on a device of some kind. While devices can be great—my classroom is mostly paperless (save for readings), and students can easily access our school's learning management system—there has been a great deal of research recently that suggests students who are able to take notes by hand have some advantages. Namely, students who handwrite have a greater capacity to synthesize the broader concepts of the material. While students on laptops are typing everything verbatim, students who are handwriting need to be more discerning and are therefore activating different parts of the their brains while writing (May, 2014). This would give a definite check mark on the pro side of handwritten notetaking as opposed to typing.

One caveat: This research seems to rely on the idea that teachers are lecturing and the students are taking notes on said lecture. I don't do a lot of lectures, so the notes that students take are structured differently. However, I think there is merit in the hand-brain connection while learning, regardless of why the notes are being taken. So I allow students to take notes in either format—handwritten or typed. I don't require everything on their devices. When we give options, we put students in the position of getting to decide for themselves what works for them at school. It's middle school, so they *should* get more autonomy and choice.

> I strongly believe that each person's brain organizes information differently. It doesn't necessarily make sense for students to use a one-size-fits-all approach to notetaking. However . . . it's better for middle school students to learn *some* way of organization before branching off to "do their own thing."

I strongly believe that each person's brain organizes information differently. It doesn't necessarily make sense for students to use a one-size-fits-all approach to notetaking. However, as is true with teaching academic essay writing, it's better for middle school students to learn *some* way of organization before branching off to "do their own thing."

To that end, my planning collaborators and I decided on a format similar to Cornell Notes. Figure 2.1 shows an example.

The Note-Taking Protocol

The column titles often change; they aren't always called "evidence" and "conclusions." But the point is that students are drawing conclusions on one

Figure 2.1 Notes Protocol

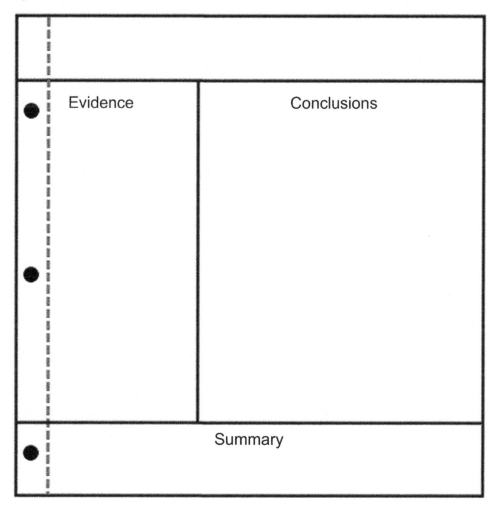

side of the paper and are backing them up with evidence on the other. The topics and headings change depending on the content of the lesson. Sometimes I will ask a question on one side (for example, "What is Tupac's view of America?"), and on the other side, students will use evidence (for example, from the song "Changes") to back up their answer. For the summary in this example, I asked students to extrapolate *why* they felt Tupac's view was what it was. Pretty quickly, this notes protocol becomes engrained in students' minds. Students get used to the idea of backing up any assertions they make with evidence—which is helpful when we get to thesis-driven writing later. The protocol also provides a platform for students to do the brainwork that might be done primarily through oral discussion. In this way, each student is responsible for thinking about the discussion question and can share with a partner, but doesn't have to necessarily share with the whole class—which would be time-consuming and inefficient for each discussion question.

This notes protocol gets used every day, unless students are in the midst of a project or their own research. The routineness of this notetaking allows for saved time (students know how to set up their notes—in fact, that is often the subject of a "Do Now"). It also gives the students some structure in terms of what to expect. This notetaking protocol is harder than having to write notes down verbatim—they have to think and synthesize information—but once they have done it a few times with success, they gain a feeling of self-efficacy. And they appreciate the predictability of format—it helps them to know that they can stretch to grapple with challenging questions and challenging content because they already know the format to use. This way, they are not trying to master two things at once.

I also help students organize the notes they take in class. Students who are not innately skilled organizers need explicit scaffolding and modeling for this. I show students how to create folders on their computers to keep all of their work from class. Or, if they are handwriting their notes, they make a table of contents with dividers for notes and other classroom miscellany. Each note page (or file, or doc) is labeled with a title of the lesson and is given a number so that students can organize their notes in a tangible or virtual folder, on their device or in the cloud. Each unit has its own folder under a larger heading of "U.S. History" or whatever the students want to title the class. I make myself available during the year, too, for students who want to work on organization—because even with setting a foundation for organization at the beginning of the year, it can be difficult to maintain. When we help students with organization, they are much more successful with it than if we just expect them to do it on their own with no coaching. For those students who are just naturally organized, or who have somehow trained themselves to be so, they can use whatever system works for them. Support and modeling, but with choice—that's the balance of middle school.

> When we help students with organization, they are much more successful with it than if we just expect them to do it on their own with no coaching.... Support and modeling, but with choice—that's the balance of middle school.

Speaking of choice: Halfway through the year, if students want to adjust their notetaking format, I allow them to do so. I want to give students both a foundation to be successful in storing and responding to information and ideas, and the autonomy to take risks and figure this stuff out for themselves.

When They Need to Do Something at Home

It's one thing for us to be demanding of middle schoolers in class, but many of us also give homework—and homework is a sticky subject depending on your philosophy. You might believe that homework should be limited or nonexistent, or that it cultivates discipline, or that it provides invaluable content review—but regardless of your personal beliefs, your decision to assign homework might also depend on the culture of the school and the philosophy of the administration.

I've tried to play both sides in terms of homework. I never want to give homework just to give it; it needs to be purposeful, not busywork. I don't usually give nightly homework, though when I do, the exception is usually reading and annotations. More often, I give projects or writing assignments that students have a few weeks to complete. With those kinds of assignments, though, students may need help setting smaller goals so they don't put off the whole project until the last minute. My students have heard my whole spiel a billion times: Think about your future self. Your future self doesn't want to do the work any more than your present self. *But*, your future self will thank your past self if you do the work now. Students laugh politely or groan or roll their eyes, but they know it's an issue. Procrastinators abound in middle school!

In terms of homework load, middle school students are stretched as it is; many are involved in extracurricular activities or have family obligations that take up their time. However, for a middle school student who may need to "practice" working and not procrastinating, regular homework can be a helpful experience in and of itself.

At my school, we use a learning management system, and each homework assignment, along with any supplementary materials, is found on the site. Though there is always discussion about whether we're being too handhold-y by making everything available to students, this learning management system is helpful for them and is a good compromise, I think. We must try to remember that these kids have just come from elementary school, and the parts of the brain that control executive functioning—including organization and logic—are not fully formed yet (Giedd, 2015). So students may, developmentally and neurologically, still *need* a bit of handholding. Anyway, they still have to *do* the work. And they don't always.

When we put information in a learning management system—or in another online, centralized place—reminders, calendars, and assignment details are fully available for students. So long as students can access the Internet, there aren't any more lost papers or calls to friends to get the assignment details. Everything is in one place. However, while this might look like we're giving too much help, the students still need to take the initiative to actually complete the assignment. And isn't that the goal? Especially in history class, where there are so many skills to work on and so much content to delve into, wouldn't we rather work on those than on straight organizational tools? Ideally, having assignments and instructions in a centralized place will allow whatever time would have been spent on organization to be spent fully on the assignment. To that end, Enrico Gnaulati posits that schools have been placing an increased emphasis on organization, compliance, and preparation, which he says alienates students who don't innately have these skills. One might extrapolate that the vast majority of middle school students whose brains are still developing organizational functioning are being asked to do more than they are neurologically ready to do (2013). So providing helpful structures and organizational tools can only be supportive for students who may or may not already have these tools. Middle school students need help getting organized and figuring out what they need to do; they also need chances to meet expectations and do the work—or not do it and learn from the consequences.

> Middle school students need help getting organized and figuring out what they need to do; they also need chances to meet expectations and do the work—or not do it and learn from the consequences.

When students don't do the work expected of them in a history class—especially in a class that is focused on collaboration, critical thinking skills, and autonomy—it is difficult for them to improve academically. Middle school isn't such a terrible time to learn that there are consequences for not doing the work, though it is arguable whether grades are a motivator for every kid. At my school, we do have a standard grading system, and on the whole, students are motivated by their grades (some too much, of course; some too little). Ideally, students would work for the sake of work and learn in order to learn, but grades are part and parcel of most of the larger educational system.

When They Earn Grades

I had an epiphany about grades when I was a sixth grader myself: I realized that I had something to do with my grades. My first real middle school report card was spotty at best, and since my image of myself was of a good, no, a *strong* student, this was crazy! I had to think: Why had this happened? Was it because my teachers didn't like me? That is what I had always chalked up any negative grades or comments to before . . . No, I realized, it was because I wasn't really *working*. Middle school was harder, and I wasn't working hard enough. That was the moment I became conscious of my academic self, the moment I realized I had some agency in my own marks and in my own academic trajectory. I wonder, now, what would have happened if I had never had that wake-up call, if there hadn't been a report that didn't jive with the way I saw and wanted to see myself. It occurs to me that the knowledge I discovered then *may* have been obvious to all of my peers, but it wasn't to me, and I have to imagine there still exist students like me all the way into eighth grade, even.

I try to remember this when my students come up to me at the end of the semester having put off thinking about or dealing with grades they weren't happy with until the last minute. They want to change their grade or know if they can have extra credit. As I explain in my syllabus and at the beginning of the year, I don't do extra credit. Yes, eighth grade may be "high stakes" for some students who want to go to elite private schools, but in general, middle school is a good time to be able to mess up, to have an epiphany that you yourself can change what needs to be changed. So many middle school students still feel like their grades are dependent on whether the teacher likes them. Realizing that their own agency has something to do with their grades is a strong lesson for them. This isn't to say that students who aren't getting "good" grades are not working up to their potential. Grades can, of course, indicate whether a student needs additional support in a particular area. But obviously, this is a different issue that should be addressed by parents, guardians, teachers, administrators, and support personnel.

In my class, if students *work*, they should be able to get at least a C, if not better. Most assignments are submitted in iterations. Improvements are made as they go, and final grades reflect that improvement. Additionally, many grades are for projects; if the students meet the expectations of the rubric, then they should be able to earn the points on the project.

Another way we can give students autonomy over their own success is by using a transparent gradebook. As soon as there are enough (at least four) grades in the online gradebook, I publish the grades on our learning management system (students can only see their individual grade) and these grades are available until grades come out. Students are never in the dark as to what they are getting. The upside of this is that students can advocate for themselves—and preferably early—if they need to ramp it up for the next assignment to get their grades where they want them to be. In addition, parents can see what the students' grades are, so there aren't any surprises at report card time.

When I was in school, it was basically a mystery how a student was doing in the classroom. You had to go to the teacher and ask, or wait for notes to periodically be sent home. This is still the case in classrooms where there isn't access to technology (either in schools or at home) or where there isn't a transparent gradebook. Students in those situations don't have the ability to do much about their grades, and they don't even understand that they *have* to do something about their grade. The student is dependent on the teacher. But in middle school, we don't want dependency; we want students to begin taking responsibility for their own learning.

When They Need to Review or Need Additional Help

Another tool that allows students to take control over their own learning and understanding is the online review video. Over the past few years, I have begun to employ, in a limited fashion, the flipped classroom model of showing videos for a few of my classroom routines. I used to be biased against the flipped classroom model and wrote about that on the MiddleWeb blog *Future of History* (www.middleweb.com/11419/confronting-flipped-classroom-bias). I originally felt that the flipped classroom model assumed classrooms were lecture- and fact-based, and didn't allow for the use of inquiry and critical-thinking strategies. However, after learning more about the model, I decided to roll it out in a *very limited* fashion. Now, I use it a bit—mostly at the beginning of the year to establish routines. For example, if students aren't sure how to set up their notes, there is a video for that. I've used both the Educreations and ShowMe apps to create whiteboard videos with my voice, along with instructions and pictures that walk students through the steps of whatever routine is in question. Students can review at their own pace in class or outside of class. I've committed to video instructions on how to complete a Body Biography (discussed in a later chapter), how and when to cite sources, how to annotate a text for class, how to set up notes, how to write a paragraph with evidence, and how to create a checklist before turning in writing assignments. These videos are meant to be concise and clear. I struggle with the concise part, but I am working on it.

When I first used videos to flip the classroom, I wasn't sure how the students would react or how it would work. I have to say that it's gone OK. Students don't *always* utilize the videos at their disposal, but the fact that they have the option of doing so makes them feel supported whether or not they choose to actually put in the time. While it's true that videos in the classroom are often, by virtue of being videos, more interesting to students than reading or other media, they get tired of them pretty quickly if they are overused (as with anything used too much!). I learned this the hard way last year when I went a little crazy with the amount of video that I used to start teaching procedures at the beginning of the year. By the end, students were rolling their eyes when I mentioned there was a "video on that." Middle schoolers are a tough audience, but they need variation and interaction in order to stay engaged. They aren't going to want to watch video after video—even if flipping the classroom does allow for more one-on-one interactions with students during class time.

Admittedly, I still feel like the flipped classroom model would work best for a history classroom where the teacher is the one presenting most of the information. So if you want to shift toward more student-centered, constructivist, or project-based lessons, the flipped model is best used sparingly. But it is great for what it's great for. If students need to watch how to create a paragraph over and over, and it helps them craft their paragraph? They can. Flipped classroom videos can allow students who work at a slower pace, or who need additional support, or who are perfectionists, to work as much as their hearts desire.

When Students Reflect on Their Own Progress

Another important routine for us to help middle school students develop is reflection. At this age, students can seem to sleepwalk through the academic parts of their schooling; they are used to being told what to do, and they don't necessarily *think* about what they are doing or what they could be doing differently. Things going wrong during group work? History is difficult? Homework feels like too much? Not understanding something happening in class? Often, middle school kids don't even really *notice* there is a problem—or if they do, they sidestep it and sweep it under the rug. Metacognition and reflection can help middle schoolers overcome this "academic unconsciousness."

> Often, middle school kids don't even really *notice* there is a problem—or if they do, they sidestep it and sweep it under the rug. Metacognition and reflection can help middle schoolers overcome this "academic unconsciousness."

Before my students do their first group work project, they reflect on how group work usually feels for them. They think about what role they usually take—whether they tend to take the lead, whether they take direction, or if they try to coast along, hoping their teammates will do the work for them. Having these conversations goes a long way in improving collaborative work, but they have to be routine. Each time they've engaged in teamwork, students need to reflect on what their contribution level was. The way I ask is: Did you do your ten points of work today? The idea is that if each team of four has a pool of 40 points, then ideally, each team member should be doing 10 points of work. If one student isn't working up to snuff one day, then his or her teammates might pick up the slack, making the breakdown look more like 6, 12, 12, 10—as long as it adds up to 40. Often these points are just theoretical; assigning them is a reflective exercise in which students think back on their progress so that they can be more aware in the moment next time. This kind of repetition helps students become more aware, and it changes their teamwork behavior over time.

Another reflective strategy I use is exit cards (or other periodic reflection devices). Exit cards are typically known as assessment tools and can be used to check students' understanding of content. However, we can also use them to help students reflect on their own learning and where they are. For example, if we are studying the expansion of the United States, I might ask students at the beginning of the unit, or midway through the unit: What is something that you are still not sure of? What is your plan to figure it out?

That is a quick way to have students get in the habit of reflection, and it also provides data for the teacher in terms of what students need to work on and how they think they might be able to improve. Then, at the end of the unit, students can reflect on what they feel they've accomplished and what they would change about their work habits for the next unit. They can discuss what they were most interested in and what they had to push themselves to think about or learn. They can delve into the "whys" as well: Why did this particular task feel more challenging than another? Why did I enjoy this one or find it easy? What kind of work do I feel I do best? What kind of work challenges me? Those questions can come at any time, and they can be specific to content or general, but no matter how you use them, they can help students think about their learning—and think about their thinking!

Students may need some modeling and scaffolding for this reflective exercise at first, because not every middle school student will be able to even identify whether there is an issue, much less be able to pinpoint what they can do to ameliorate it. But practice makes for improvement, and this kind of reflective practice can be beneficial in any discipline, not just in history.

Why Routines in Middle School?

Middle school, is, well, in the middle. In elementary school, students expect their teachers to do a certain amount of handholding when it comes to planning and organizational skills. Middle schoolers often experience a big jump in responsibility between fifth and sixth grade, despite their underdeveloped prefrontal cortex (the part of the brain in charge of executive functioning like organization, logic, predicting routine, planning ahead, etc.). In some ways, we throw students into a more high-school centered world and hope that they swim instead of sink. However, as middle school teachers, we should set routines to help the classroom function smoothly—and even more importantly, to help students build their executive functioning skills.

Don't forget that we are asking students to focus on these skills while they are in a hotbed of hormonal shifts, as well as neurological and developmental social and emotional turmoil (or "messy growth," you could call it). Students have to navigate the new social scene, find their place within it, and figure out all of their new feelings; they hardly have time to work on school stuff. Routines, then, help students to experience a bit of predictability in a sea of unpredictability. Additionally, routines, especially those that encourage critical thinking and reflective metacognition, can help students develop habits that will aid them in growing and stretching their executive functioning skills—including the habit of thinking *about* their own thinking. They don't know what they don't know yet, and they might not be parsing the academic parts of their lives in the way they are parsing the social and emotional parts. They need all the chances they can get to learn to advocate for themselves and their grades, to reflect on their teamwork, to learn new strategies for learning, and to reflect on their own learning trajectory. It is our job, then, as middle school teachers, to create predictable and routine classroom events that can help students eventually figure out and develop their own skills.

Chapter 2 Self-Reflection

1. What structures and routines do you use in your classroom to maximize time?
2. How are students emotionally supported by the routines you choose?
3. What strategies from this chapter are you thinking of utilizing?
4. What adjustments might you need to make to these strategies in order to use them in your own classroom and meet the needs of your own students?

References

Giedd, Jay N. "Risky Teen Behavior Is Driven by an Imbalance in Brain Development." *Scientific American Global RSS*. N.p., June 2015. Web. 27 July 2015.

Gnaulati, Enrico. *Back to Normal: Why Ordinary Childhood Behavior Is Mistaken for ADHD, Bipolar Disorder, and Autism Spectrum Disorder*. Boston: Beacon Press, 2013. E-book.

May, Cindi. "A Learning Secret: Don't Take Notes with a Laptop." *Scientific American Global RSS*. N.p., 3 June 2014. Web. 11 Aug. 2015.

3

Comprehension and Analysis of Expository Texts in History

What Does It Say? What Does It Mean?

When I sat down to plan U.S. History curriculum with fellow teacher Aaron Brock, we knew we wanted to use reading comprehension strategies. From both personal experience *and* teaching experience, we knew that students struggle to read expository text, and when they *can* technically decode the words in front of them, they often struggle to engage with the text enough to comprehend.

This presents a problem for history class, where almost all of the text is expository. In fact, friends have told me that they didn't like history class when they were younger because of the type and amount of reading. And while there may be some parts of how history class was taught in the past that should be adjusted—like the "lecture and answer the questions in the back of the book" model—the reading part is imperative and should not go by the wayside. Nevertheless, we can analyze and finesse how we approach it with students so that students can get as much as possible out of a text and gain comprehension tools along the way. I don't teach from the textbook, though I do use it sometimes. Instead, I usually write text for students to read, and I use various primary and secondary sources to accompany it; that's what my students cut their historical expository teeth on.

What *Is* Expository Text?

Before showing students the annotation strategy that they would spend so much time on during the year, I first started by doing a "Concept Attainment" activity (see Figure 3.1). In this strategy, students work with the properties of ideas before looking at the idea itself; it is a strategy borrowed from the scientific method, using logic and contrast in order to help define ideas based on analysis of their properties. Often, positive exemplars are used on one side and the opposite, or close to it, on the other. To help elucidate the concept of expository text, I gathered examples of fiction books, poems, newspapers, historical texts, secondary sources, and words and phrases like inform/entertain, plot and conflict, and maps and sidebars. Then I had the students separate them into two columns: Column A (fiction/non-expository text) and Column B (expository text). Once the students grouped them according to characteristics of expository text, I finally gave them the label to affix to column B: "Expository Text." Students then came up with their own definition of expository text based on the characteristics in that column. I had a student last year who was so excited that he understood the concept of expository text. He went around the classroom in search of books and kept holding them up: "This one is expository! This one, too! This one isn't!" He had to feel the books and continue the sorting in a more tangible

Figure 3.1 Concept Attainment

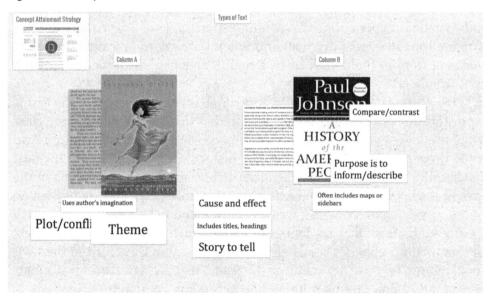

way, but he *got* the concept. In that way, it was a strength that expository text was presented as a dichotomy, too; while of course there are nuances in text and texts that defy categorization, when explaining a challenging concept, sometimes it's easiest to be able to classify into a "yes" or "no" category. This certainly seemed to work with my students.

I believe strongly in the power of honesty with middle schoolers. Once we've gotten a definition for expository text, it's always time for some real talk about how they *feel* about reading expository texts. There's something funny about kids: They are so honest a lot of the time, but they don't like to let their teachers down. They feel like they are the only ones who think that expository text can be mind-numbingly boring—they think somehow they might be disappointing the teacher with this truth. But try to get them to talk about it; once they do, they realize that when they are struggling to read expository texts, it isn't because there's something wrong with *them*. It's because the text is not always written in the most exciting way, or because the vocabulary used is often challenging, or dry, or because it's a format that takes *practice* to engage with and comprehend. This is not to say that all expository text is boring; I wouldn't be a history teacher if *I* didn't enjoy reading (some) expository text, but it is important with middle school students to allow for the reality that reading expository text isn't necessarily their number one favorite thing—and it *can* be boring sometimes.

It is also in this way that I introduce the annotations strategy: Because students don't always love the tedium of annotating, I want to make sure that they know *why* they are doing what they are doing. So many of them admit that they tune out when they read expository texts and can't remember what they'd read for pages; I let them know that this strategy makes it so that they can't just tune out and stop focusing while reading, but yes, it is time-consuming and does require their focus.

And I make sure to tell my students that they aren't the only ones who need support with reading expository text. Adults, students, everyone benefits from strategies for reading. Berkeley and Riccomini (2013) found that students who were able to use a comprehension monitoring strategy were better able to understand what they read—this applied to both students with special needs and students in general education classes. Students having a metacognitive understanding of whether they are understanding what they read can be invaluable—it brings them into their own reading experience and gives them agency. They are in charge of whether they can understand the text or not and, if not, what they can do about it. Additionally, Tejero Hughes and Parker-Katz (2013) say that just the inclusion of reading strategies will help students with learning disabilities to be able to better understand what they read. The strategy itself may not be as important as the fact that students are *equipped* with strategies.

Students do groan occasionally when they have to annotate something, but I've also had students begrudgingly, or not so begrudgingly, admit to me that doing annotations has changed the way they read: They can better attend because they are engaging with the text.

If there's anything I've learned about middle school students, it's that they don't like doing the same thing over and over again, so I don't make them do the same reading comprehension strategy each time they read an expository text. Sometimes they annotate, sometimes they do QAR (Question Answer Relationship), and other times I will have them look for something to bring in based on the reading—a point of interest or a question.

There are many reading strategies out there, all designed to help students glean the most important information from a text and figure out what it means.

Survey of Expository Text Strategies

Why so many reading strategies? And which are the best? This isn't a cut and dried question, unfortunately, and there are a lot of really strong strategies that work well with middle school students. Each has its own purpose and goal, and you can use one or more in your classroom, depending on your needs. Social Studies School Service (www.socialstudies.com), located in Culver City, California, is an amazing resource for educators; if you don't live in the Los Angeles area, they have a comprehensive website with social studies materials and texts for teachers. One of their published resources, *Strategic Reading in U.S. History* (Heafner and Massey, 2006), condenses many of these reading strategies, which, despite its title, can be used for *any* social studies content area or other disciplines, for that matter.

Knowing the Purpose for Reading

One of the first strategies described in the book is a metacognitive one, asking the students to identify exactly what they need to read for. Is it a multiple choice test? Discussion? Essay? And for each type of purpose, the authors identify a strategy for the students to use that will help them reach their purpose most effectively. For example, if the student needs to be ready for a discussion, the authors suggest that he or she put Post-Its with questions on each page that they read. Conversely, if the student needs to prepare for a multiple choice test, the student should concentrate on the 5Ws (Who, What, When, Where, and Why). Students can use this strategy for reading in any discipline. Do you usually have students read for class discussion or for essay prompts? Then have the conversation or create a chart for the students to refer back to—explaining what the purpose of their reading is and what strategies they could use in order to be successful based on that particular purpose. The idea is that students who are *aware* of what they will need to do with the expository text and are armed with strategies that work accordingly will be better prepared for class, will be better able to sort through all the extra information in text, and will then be more confident readers.

> Students who are *aware* of what they will need to do with the expository text and are armed with strategies that work accordingly will be better prepared for class, will be better able to sort through all the extra information in text, and will then be more confident readers.

Monitoring Comprehension

Another strategy Heafner and Massey suggest is to have the students monitor their own comprehension as they read. Most of the time, students have a vague notion that they don't (or do) understand what they are reading, but they aren't *really* thinking about it. If they did start paying more attention to their understanding, students would be engaging in metacognition. If students think about what they are thinking about as they read, they will be better able to identify whether they need assistance with the expository text they are reading. The authors suggest that students should ask themselves whether they can summarize what they have read in a few sentences. If they can't, they need to go back and reread. This is a novel concept for middle schoolers, as many students' conceptions of reading is of the "get it done" variety, not the "read thoroughly" variety. Students are looking to read as quickly as possible. Often, the concept of rereading doesn't even occur to them. According to Heafner and Massey, the students can simply ask themselves if they can explain in a few sentences what they are reading after every page or so in order to continue to monitor their comprehension. They need to ask themselves if the text seems to make sense to them. If it doesn't, they will need to . . . wait for it . . . reread. Unfortunately for the students, this strategy may end up highlighting just how often students need to reread to clarify the meaning of text. It may behoove the teacher, and by proxy the students, to be very transparent here. I know that when I am reading a challenging expository text, there are times, either because of the text difficulty or because I've spaced out for some reason, that I wouldn't be able to summarize what the text was saying in a few sentences. Students need to know that they're not alone in needing assistance when reading expository text; adults reread too when they aren't sure what the text is saying. This strategy doesn't necessarily provide a way for students to engage *with* the text while they read, but it definitely helps students to be more aware of their own understanding while they read. As a result, this strategy can also be used in conjunction with other strategies.

> Students need to know that they're not alone in needing assistance when reading expository text; adults reread too when they aren't sure what the text is saying.

Using Visual Imagery to Help with Textual Understanding

With this strategy, Heafner and Massey suggest that students break up the text into chunks and use visual imagery to guide students' reading through each text chunk. For example, the student has read, say, a paragraph of a text. The student then sketches a picture based on what they read. They identify the words and phrases that led them to draw that picture. Then they repeat for each chunk. The authors suggest a three-columned table (see Table 3.1) that includes the visual image, the words and phrases, and a final column that has students check their image to see if their visual image was "correct"—after they've read the entire selection (all of the chunks).

This helps students to concretize auditory or written text into a visual representation (which will speak to some students' strengths) and then to

Table 3.1 Using Visual Imagery to Help with Textual Understanding

Visual Image	Words and Phrases	Check your Image. Was it correct?

think about why they've drawn what they've drawn. Then later, the students go back and check their visual inferences against the text itself. This strategy requires multi-leveled engagement with the text: Students need to think about what they are reading enough to be able to put it into a picture; they need to be able to match that picture to the text itself with the words and phrases component; and finally, they need to be able to go back into the text and check their images to make sure that by the end of the entire text, they were correct in terms of each component of their visual image. By the end, the students will have worked so intensely with the text, that even students who aren't inclined or helped by adding a visual component should still have a strong understanding of what the text is about. Students can also benefit from the chunking strategy—both in terms of lowering their own possible anxiety about reading larger sections of expository text, and also as a strategy that they can self-employ when confronted with a large swath of expository text.

Cause and Effect

History is a discipline that includes a lot of cause and effect, so it is natural that Heafner and Massey include a cause and effect strategy in their book. With this strategy, students can use a chart similar to the one I use, which I call the "notetaking protocol" in Chapter 2—the double entry/ Cornell-type notes. For this chart, students would place the label "Cause" on the left and "Effect" on the right side. This exercise is deceptively easy in that, at first glance, it looks easier than other expository text strategies, but it's not actually as easy as it looks. It may be a pretty basic strategy: Students go through a history text—whatever it may be—and identify effects and then what caused them, or they identify causes and then what the effects of those causes were. You can see that there are multiple ways of looking at how to do this particular strategy, and in each, students will have to do a great deal of engaging with and critical thinking about the text.

I wouldn't use this strategy for just any expository text about history, but for one where cause and effect is particularly relevant. For example, because Napoleon lost his Haitian colony to rebellion, he sold the Louisiana Territory to the United States. Because of the Louisiana Purchase, there was a huge westward migration and because of the westward migration, countless Native American tribes were removed from their homes. Westward migration also led to new states wanting to come into the Union, which increased tensions about slavery. Then, America began/continued to fight within itself about territory, politics, and slaves. This kind of cause and effect chain would be something that would lend itself to this strategy. Or perhaps a class could look at the effect of Genghis Khan and the invasion of the Mongols on Chinese culture and philosophy, or the effects of Henry VIII's divorce of Catherine of Aragon and how it affected religion and politics. Most texts don't clearly delineate what exactly is cause and effect, so Heafner and Massey suggest that students look for clue words such as "because," "as a result," "this led to," "since," "subsequently," "consequently," etc. Identifying causes and their effects is just another example of a strategy that will heighten students' awareness of what they are reading and hopefully give them some skills that they can apply when they read any text, not just expository and not just in history class.

Pick One or Two Strategies: You Don't Want to Confuse Things

Each expository text comprehension strategy has a place and purpose, but it isn't necessarily going to be the best thing for your students if you use every single one at all times. Using a strategy, and learning how and when to apply it, is a skill in and of itself. Students need time to be able to *learn* the strategy. It would be difficult to ask them to use a new one constantly, as they would have to be able to work on reading, learning the strategy, *and* understanding content all at the same time. That's fine when learning a new strategy at the beginning of the year, or once in a while to break things up and help students who might be struggling with a particular skill, but it isn't something you want to throw at middle schoolers all the time.

Until a few years ago, I was loathe to use more than one reading strategy a year really, as I was worried I was asking students to gain mastery of the strategy itself to the detriment of the reading comprehension. However, I realized that you can have a couple in your back pocket and that students can master a few strategies and be able to apply them at various times depending on need. I won't underestimate my students like that again. However, I think the concern is valid. You don't want your students to be worrying about whether they are doing the format exactly right. They should *know* the format, and then they will be on autopilot for that part, and, in theory, focusing on the content and the reading itself while employing the engagement tools of the strategy. To that end, these next two strategies are the ones that I chose to focus on in my own history classroom.

QAR (Question Answer Relationship)

One of the first reading strategies that Aaron and I decided on using in our first few meetings was QAR (Raphael, 1986). It's a leveled questioning reading strategy that helps students to discern four different information types that go with four question types.

Level 1: Right There: The answer to this question will be in the text in one place and could likely be quoted verbatim. Hands down, if you polled middle school students, this is the easiest question.

Level 2: Think and Search: The answer to this question will be in the text, but in a couple different places. These are easy to answer, but they are really hard, for some reason, to come up with.

Levels 1 and 2 make up the information in the text that is explicit. Levels 3 and 4 are more inferential. This is when the labels get slightly vague.

Level 3: The Author and You: This is basically an inferential question. The author might imply something based on the text, but the answer isn't *in* the text. There can be multiple answers for a level three. These aren't so difficult once students get the hang of them.

Level 4: On Your Own: Half of my students find these easy, while the other half find them incredibly challenging. I think the demarcation is developmental and goes back to Piaget: The students who find this type of question "easy" are further along in their Formal Operational Stage and will be able to do this kind of abstract thinking; those who find it difficult are still more in the Concrete Operational Stage (Piaget and Inhelder, 1969). Level 4 questions ask the reader to take the specific details out of a text and extrapolate the larger themes such that readers could ask anyone on the street and get their thoughts. For example: If students are reading about the Constitutional Convention, a teacher could ask: Who should make the rules for a country? This takes the specifics out and formulates the question based on a broader theme covered in the text.

QAR can be challenging to teach, and it takes students awhile to get used to the differences between question types. Another issue is that when students are tasked to come up with QAR questions themselves, they can get so distracted trying to get their assigned quota of questions that they will rush through the reading and devise questions that don't have a lot of substance behind them. There are checks and balances one can employ to mitigate these issues, however, such as requiring at least one question per page or at least two from the last page, that kind of thing. Students need to read the selection through first before searching for questions, and questions need to pass the "is this important?" test. The metacognition that this strategy can allow is very helpful in all disciplines. The language of knowing which types of information are found in text can be invaluable. I will hear students say to each other, "Well, for that question, you won't find it in the text; it's a level 3."

Additionally, having students come up with the questions themselves can be more empowering than the teacher simply finding the most important information and crafting the questions him- or herself. The questions that an individual student or team comes up with can be exchanged with other individuals or teams for further engagement with a particular text.

> Students who are reading the text and coming up with their own questions to engage with the text are less passive and more active in the process of their own learning.

It was hard to feel any agency when I read and had to answer the questions in the back of the book when *I* was in eighth grade. Students who are reading the text and coming up with their own questions to engage with the text are less passive and more active in the process of their own learning.

Annotation Strategy

After using QAR, Aaron was looking for an even more rigorous way for his students to be able to read and comprehend text. Often, students can struggle with reading the text itself, not just comprehending it. To this end, he created, and we both employed in the classroom, an annotation strategy that worked with the idea of the 5 Ws: Who, What, When, Where, Why.

Students would then take the annotations that they worked on and create a page of notes in which they synthesized the information they found into ideas and into their own words. This part took a great deal of practice and was both challenging and time-consuming:

Reading Notes Instructions

1. Set up notes (this is with the usual notes format discussed in Chapter 2).
2. Use the current unit and the title of the text you just annotated as the title of the notes.

3. Put your first main idea on the left side of the notes.
4. Summarize everything you underlined about that main idea on the right side of the notes.
5. Repeat Steps 3 and 4 with each of your main ideas.
6. Write an objective summary at the end of the notes.
7. The objective summary must include all 5 Ws.

While this particular strategy takes a while for the students to complete, once they do end up mastering the format, it helps tremendously when students are reading expository text. They understand the most important parts of the text and main concepts. From there, we can do more complicated historiography, comparisons of sources, and evaluation. But in order to do critical thinking at all, students have to understand and comprehend both what the text is about and the concepts themselves. This type of strategy goes a long way in setting up a foundation of basic understanding of the text so that students must comprehend before continuing. It's this strategy that I have received positive feedback about, where students have come in the next day and told me that they'd never really understood how to read text before (especially expository text) and that this helped them to *actually* comprehend what they were reading.

Learning How to Paraphrase

Annotation Instructions*:

1. Look for **four** main ideas that will eventually go into your notes.
2. Each main idea must be one of the 5 Ws.

   a. **Who**: names, groups of people
   b. **When**: years, time periods

c. **Where**: places, regions

d. **What**: events, ideas

e. **Why**: causes, motivations

3. <u>Underline every sentence</u> where you find your main ideas.

4. In the margin, label each underlined sentence with the name of the main idea.

*Used with permission from Aaron Brock

One of the logical next steps from reading expository text is to paraphrase it—put what is read in different words for research, notes, or another purpose. Students often struggle with paraphrasing the expository text that they read. It is a skill to be able to paraphrase, and many students need explicit help, not just in learning how to do it, but in learning that they *have* to paraphrase and can't just rip small parts—or large parts—of text from a source and pass it off as their own. I discuss in more detail the mental gymnastics that students need to do in order to realize that citations are necessary in the first place in Chapter 5, but paraphrasing and citations are close relatives. When students read expository text for the purpose of gleaning information about it to use for, say, research purposes, I suggest that they read a sentence, think about what has been said and write it down simply. Some of the mental block that students have about paraphrasing is this feeling that they will never be able to say the sentence better than it has originally been written; they don't want their sentence to be "less than" the original, so they use as many words from the original sentence as possible. Part of helping students learn how to paraphrase is to give them the permission to write a sentence that sounds like something *they'd* write. They don't have to sound like adults yet, but they should sound like they understand what they've written.

> It is a skill to be able to paraphrase, and many students need explicit help, not just in learning how to do it, but in learning that they *have* to paraphrase.

Another tactic students use is to just change one or two words, or change most of the words of the sentence into synonyms, but keep the sentence structure and meaning exactly the same. This can be a little dangerous—synonyms for one thing aren't always enough to convey the original intent of the sentence, and may change the meaning in a slight, but significant way. Additionally, keeping the sentence structure exactly the same isn't showing that the student understands the actual meaning of the sentence, but rather that they have facility with the online thesaurus or that they can change a few words here and there. Again, this is actually a good step. If students are at this level and are changing most of the words in a sentence, they at least know that they shouldn't be copying it word for word and that it needs to be paraphrased. But to truly paraphrase means to express the gist of an idea in your own way; this is what they need help and "permission" to do. The two main suggestions I give are to practice reading a few sentences (better than just one), looking away from the text, thinking about what the excerpt means and *then* writing it down (still without looking) in the student's words. Then they can look back at the text to make sure the meaning is clear and true to the original. They need practice and reminders with this. And one of the most important things they need to remember is that their words, not anyone else's, are what's important. If they can't say it (yet) as beautifully as a historian who has been writing his or her whole adult life, well, that makes sense. They just need to be truthful, honest, and do their best work. Their *own* clear writing is what they should be aspiring to.

It is implicit in the idea of paraphrasing that students need to be able to *understand* what they read. This is one of the reasons why the Annotation Notes described above include both an objective summary that comes at the end of the reading, as well as summaries of the main ideas. These summaries should be in the students' own words and are good practice for learning how to paraphrase. Students can't paraphrase until they understand what they are reading, so both skills go hand in hand.

Putting It All Together: Why Expository Text in Middle School History?

History texts are, by virtue of being written in order to inform, almost primarily expository. Middle school students, unless they happen to be predisposed to the subject, are going to need some support in reading these kinds of texts. Otherwise, students can spend their entire middle school experience doing the sleepwalk-read—you know, the kind of reading where you've read the whole page and can't remember a thing you read because you're thinking about your grocery list or what you're going to do after work. Or, if you are in middle school, you're thinking about things that are *way* more important to you: what so-and-so said during passing period, who you're going to sit with during lunch, whether your friend still likes you, the fight you had with your parents that morning . . . middle school stuff. So for this age, in order to comprehend history class at all, middle school students are going to need strategies to help pull them into reading the expository texts that are, and should continue to be, an essential part of class.

These strategies themselves usually help students to be better readers of expository text, regardless of which one is used. This seems to speak to a strength in the students having strategies and having the agency to be able to engage with text actively. And it's not enough for students to just be able to read text; ideally, they will do something with what they read. They will need to be able to read expository texts and comprehend them in order to be able to write, to paraphrase, and to work on projects. Even project-based learning inquiry units or lessons have elements of reading expository text; students need to be able to read in order to engage in inquiry, conduct research, and create projects and presentations that show what they've learned. In a way then, reading comprehension is the foundation of history class. Students need this skill to be able to interact with history both in the past, as well as with history that is currently being made—current events cannot be comprehended fully unless a student can really dig in and read and understand text. Whether they are reading online or through an actual physical text, middle school students still need scaffolding and help to read the texts. But, the texts *are* paramount.

Chapter 3 Self-Reflection

1. What comprehension strategies do you currently use to help your students read and understand expository text?
2. When do you require close reading vs. a more perfunctory approach with expository text?
3. What strategies from this chapter are you thinking of utilizing?
4. What adjustments might you need to make for your own classroom and the needs of your students?

References

Berkeley, Sheri, and Paul J. Riccomini. "QRAC-The-Code: A Comprehension Monitoring Strategy for Middle School Social Studies Textbooks." *Journal of Learning Disabilities* 46.2 (2013): 154–165. *ERIC*. Web. 22 Aug. 2015.

Heafner, Tina, and Dixie Massey. *Strategic Reading in U.S. History.* Culver City, CA: Social Studies School Service, 2006. Print.

Piaget, Jean, and Bärbel Inhelder. *The Psychology of the Child.* New York: Basic Books, 1969. Print.

Raphael, T.E. "Teaching Question-Answer Relationships." *The Reading Teacher*, 39 (1986): 516–520.

Tejero Hughes, Marie, and Michelle Parker-Katz. "Integrating Comprehension Strategies into Social Studies Instruction." *Social Studies* 104.3 (2013): 93–104. *Psychology and Behavioral Sciences Collection.* Web. 22 Aug. 2015.

4

Evaluation of Text

What's the Perspective?

So what do we do once students can understand a text? What next? The previous chapter was all about helping students read and comprehend to see what the text *says*. In this chapter, we'll look at what students can do with the text *after* they've read and understood it. This is important because historiography—examining *how* history has been written—requires higher-level thinking than just reading and understanding something. Middle schoolers engaged in historiography will need to really think about *why* the text says what it says, how it connects to the larger themes of history, how it connects to people's ideas of the world, and how history has been used to advance ideology.

Why Historiography?

Teaching historiography is complex and fraught with choice: what to include, what to omit, whose voice to focus on, whose side to feature. There are dominant and alternative narratives of particular historical events, as well as multiple interpretations of the importance of the people and events in history.

This naturally results in a plethora of historical narratives about a particular topic—sometimes the same, sometimes varied only slightly, sometimes varied a great deal, sometimes with an agenda, and sometimes attempting to be free of a particular bias or perspective. Middle school students are surprised to hear this. Often they've been exposed to only one particular narrative of an event—that of the history textbook—which usually attempts to be bias-free. But the idea that there can be multiple perspectives on the same event is often a novel concept for students—and not an unwelcome one. We should show students that one of the interesting things about history *is* this ambiguity, this "mystery." When students think that there is actually something real to discuss, discover, or decide about history, they are much more invested in the study of the topic. Any ambiguity, any lack of clarity, any seeming skewing of events excites those parts of their brains that crave drama. And better to get it in through history than through *actual* conflict.

> The idea that there can be multiple perspectives on the same event is often a novel concept for students—and not an unwelcome one. We should show students that one of the interesting things about history *is* this ambiguity, this "mystery."

Learning to Compare Sources

The Inquiry Chart, or I-Chart for short, is another helpful resource from Heafner and Massey's *Strategic Reading in U.S. History* (2006). It's a format I recommend using when having students compare two (or possibly more) different sources. Note that when students—especially younger students—compare sources, it is best to make sure that the sources are disparate enough that there *are* some significant differences that they can observe and note. Once students have become familiar with the inquiry format, they can move to the more challenging work of comparing sources that are more similar and have fewer distinctions between them.

The I-Chart format is mostly straightforward. Students look at two different texts on the same topic (either primary or secondary sources) and compare each source's take on the event (see Table 4.1). The way they do this is by looking at what each source says about a topic, theme, historical figure, or idea about the incident. For example, when I have students compare Howard Zinn's take on Shays' Rebellion vs. Paul Johnson's take on the same event, I have them look at what each text says about the reasons for rebellion, which historical figures each text mentions were involved, whether the government's reactions are mentioned and what they were, and what each text mentions were the results of Shays' Rebellion.

The Howard Zinn excerpt comes from his *Young People's History of the United States* (2007) and Paul Johnson's is from *A History of the American People* (1998). Each of these texts has a particular viewpoint about government, America, and its people. The texts are not diametrically opposed, but they have different-enough purposes that students can see two disparate accounts of the same event. For example, Zinn's account focuses on Daniel Shays and the farmers with him who are rebelling against the government because of what they perceive as unfair taxes and jailing for unpaid debts. Zinn focuses on the reasons for those debts, explaining that they largely had to do with the government not paying promised funds to its soldiers after the Revolution, and sides with the farmers and their cause. Students do notice this, from both the I-Chart exercise and from the subsequent discussion on the perspectives of Zinn vs. Johnson.

The Johnson excerpt, on the other hand, while shorter, focuses on the rowdiness of the rebels and the difficulties that the rebellion, led by its "bankrupt" leader, made for the "practical" men in government. Students need to do a more careful and subtle read to see Johnson's perspective, but the I-Chart helps them figure it out—particularly where it asks for the names of the figures involved. That shows students the difference between the two historians' perspectives: Johnson mostly mentions the government figures *affected* by the rebellion, and the negative characteristics of those in rebellion, while Zinn mentions the protesters by name and gives them agency and cause, and even vilifies, to a certain extent, those in the government whom he sees as persecuting the farmers.

From this comparison and ones like it, students start to see that it's not only the players who have different perspectives and ways of looking at an event—the historians who are studying the event do too. And why *do* historians have different takes on an event? This can be a good thing to discuss; you can talk about how people's political views and ideas about government can be factors. Additionally, you can discuss how the circumstances of people's lives, where they are from, and what they have experienced often play a role in how they might interpret historical events. Having this kind of conversation helps students be more metacognitive about what might be in their own backpack of perspective.

When students analyze historians' writing in such a way, it helps them think critically about to their own writing in history class. For example, last year, while reading Zinn and Johnson, one of my students said, "I see why you don't want us to say 'I think'—you just want us to say it like it's true—like they do." Students see the value in supporting their thesis with evidence, but

Table 4.1 Inquiry Chart

Topic: **Shays' Rebellion**	Reasons for Rebellion	People involved	Reactions from Government	Results	Other differences
Source 1: Howard Zinn: Farmers in Revolt					

Source 2:
Excerpt from Paul
    Johnson's
    A History of the
    American People					

Conclusions: What were some major differences that you found? What do you think the reasons were for these differences? What does this tell you about Shays' Rebellion?					

they also see that they—as historians themselves—get to pick and choose the evidence that best supports their thesis. After all, that's what historians do.

You've Compared Sources, But So What?

The original I-Chart has students compare sources, but I added a part at the bottom that asks students to analyze what the differences between the two texts show about that particular event, about the historian's purpose for writing, or about history in general. This is often a new way of thinking for students. They are used to thinking that history is one narrative. Through source comparisons, they realize that there are many stories and many different people telling them. They begin to understand that they can add their own voices to the interpretation.

Let's Talk about Perspective

Lunchroom Fight

Stanford History Education Group (SHEG) has amazing resources for teaching historiography and "thinking like a historian." One of their lessons for showing students about historiography and perspective is based on a particular incident—a "lunchroom fight." (Like all of their lesson plans, it is fully fleshed out on their site sheg.stanford.edu.) The lunch-room fight is a topic that many students can relate to and that connects to their own experiences in a more tangible way than the study of the Conquistadors or something else far removed from their lives. SHEG puts forth this scenario:

> Imagine you are the principal of a school and you've just found out there was a fight in the lunchroom during lunch. You've asked many students and teachers who witnessed the fight to write down what they saw and who they think started the fight. Unfortunately, you have received many conflicting accounts that disagree about important details of the fight, like who started it, when it started, and who was involved. It's important to remember that NO ONE is lying.

Students then deconstruct the scenario, trying to figure out how there could be conflicting accounts of the exact same incident. Students mention the usual things—like position of the witnesses, people coming in at different points in the fight, and people misinterpreting actions. For example, someone trying to break up the fight could mistakenly be suspected of being an aggressor. But middle school students are also very canny; they will say things like, "well, it depends who your friends are. Maybe people aren't lying, but if your friend is one of the people involved, you're going to think it wasn't their fault, because you know the whole backstory." This is an important observation for students not only because it helps them connect their day to day to what they've learning but also because it can be applied to history in an astute way. One of the reasons that SHEG's curriculum—and specifically this lunchroom fight scenario—is so helpful for introducing historiography to students is that historiography, though daunting, is not necessarily more complicated than the machinations of middle school emotional and social politics. Students may have trouble delving into the different perspectives of those involved in the French Revolution, but they can definitely talk about the hierarchy and politics of their school! So if we approach historiography through a lens that they can relate to—not just in terms of the surface level (Hey! They have a lunch-room and we have a lunchroom, too!), but also in terms of the unspoken and unseen alliances and political factors that shape students' perspective on their own middle school experience—it makes teaching historical perspectives a bit easier.

Primary and Secondary Sources

As we've seen, it's not difficult for students to imagine that eyewitnesses to an event may see it in different ways: after all, that's their life. There's conflict in middle school, people take sides, and the sides are based on who their friends are, what happened, who did what to whom, etc. So the idea that, say, a slave and senator in Ancient Greece might have two very different perspectives on Ancient Greece is not anathema to them. However, the idea that *historians* have differing perspectives is definitely new information for these middle schoolers. They have not spent a great deal of time examining a particular historical event through different source texts, nor are they even aware that different sources would *have* different perspectives on the same event. This is why it is really important to differentiate primary and secondary sources and introduce that vocabulary to students.

Secondary Source Narrative/Life Puzzle Assignment

Students need to be able to distinguish between the account of someone who witnessed or *experienced* an event, and writings that were done about the event *after* it happened. This can be a hard concept for a middle schooler to grasp at first. I will talk in more detail about the Secondary Source Narrative/Life Puzzle Activity in Chapter 6, but this activity is one of the main ways that I have students uncover and work with the differences between a primary and secondary source. In this project, students use documents from my own life—my birth certificate, pictures, letters, diplomas, etc.—as evidence to then craft a secondary source narrative *about* my life. During the process, I make sure to use the terms "primary source documents" and "secondary source narrative" over and over so students can hear the terms used in context before having to define them themselves. From my phrasing, students are able to see the delineation between things that are *from* the time period in question and things that are written *about* the time period in question.

In addition to teaching students to differentiate between primary and secondary sources, this activity also helps students see that the interpretation of the primary sources depends on how much information is available and how much analysis and extrapolation the historian is willing to do on a particular piece of evidence, and that historians don't always have the whole picture. Students write secondary source narratives about my life, but they can see that each of their accounts contains differences. And we discuss: "What accounts for these differences? You were all looking at the same primary source documents." Each student brings his or her own backpack of experience to the process of analysis. Students look through their own lens—thin as the lens may be, since they are still so young—and interpret based on their own understandings and experiences. When they examine the differences between the secondary source narratives they created and my own biography, as well as the differences between each other's narratives, they see that history is an *interpretation* based on evidence. This is an exciting and liberating realization for history class because it leaves room for the students themselves—they can be historians, too. They just need to gain interpretive skills.

Perspective and Bias in Text

But to back up a bit: one way we can help students see that any historical event *has* multiple interpretations is to teach explicitly what bias and perspective can look like when historians are writing. Students might not realize that they know what *perspective* is, and they may need to learn the word *bias*. (Sometimes it can be better to use the word perspective because of the intensely negative connotations that the word bias can have—besides, we don't want students to assume they don't have to read something just because it's biased—but I do use both terms interchangeably.)

Introductions through Music

The first thing I do to introduce perspective and the idea that there can be different views on something is to play two different songs about America. Songs are such a strong way to hook students in and help them to remember bigger ideas. I play Tupac's "Changes" and Charlie Daniels Band's "In America." Through these two selections, students are asked to listen and, using the notes protocol described in Chapter 2, use evidence from the text—in this case, the song—to come up with a conclusion about how each artist feels about America (see Figure 4.1). Students then begin looking at how two different artists express different views on the same topic. And since we do this during a unit about the inclusivity/exclusivity of the creation of the Constitution, examining different views about America is apt.

Test before You Trust

Common Sense Media (https://www.commonsensemedia.org), a San Francisco-based company known for reviewing media so that parents, teachers, and kids can make more informed choices, also creates curriculum

Figure 4.1 Different Views of America Chart

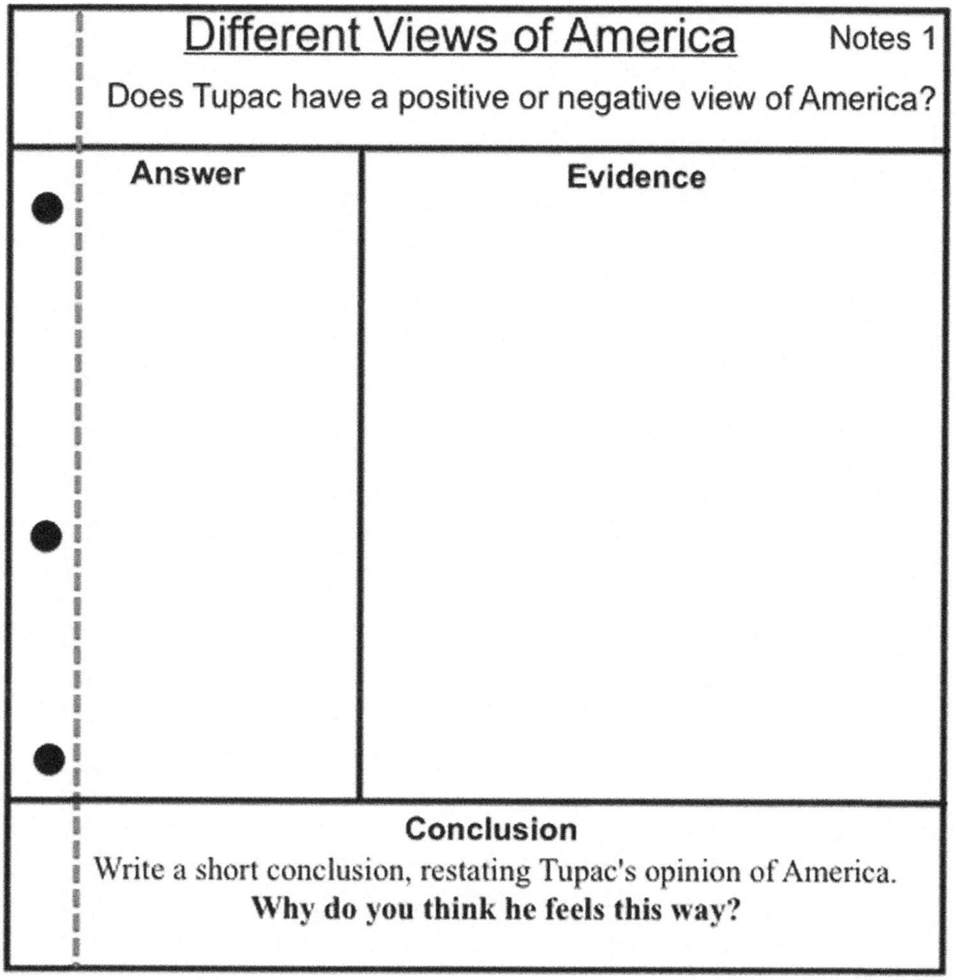

Different Views of America	Notes 1
Does Tupac have a positive or negative view of America?	

Answer	Evidence

Conclusion
Write a short conclusion, restating Tupac's opinion of America.
Why do you think he feels this way?

for teachers. One of their lesson sets is about digital literacy—specifically, analyzing websites.

They have a multiple-point checklist that students can use to test the value of a particular website through various criteria (see Table 4.2). This is a tool that I use with my students during the year even prior to discussing bias and perspective. Before students research anything for class, we go through this checklist, and students select five criteria to use when deciding whether

Table 4.2 Test Before You Trust

Purpose of the Site	Circle one	Add details to explain
1. Can you tell if the site is fact or opinion? (If the information seems one-sided, or biased, you will have to go elsewhere to hear the other side of the issue.)	**YES NO**	
2. Is the site free of advertising?	**YES NO**	
3. If there are ads, is it easy to tell the difference between ads and content?	**YES NO**	
4. Is the site sponsored by any organizations?	**YES NO**	
5. Is it clear who the site is for? (for example, college students or young children)	**YES NO**	
6. Is the tone calm and fair? (Sites that are mean and angry may not be good sources of information.)	**YES NO**	
7. Is the site open to everyone? (no age requirements, fees, passwords, or registration)	**YES NO**	
8. Is the site's domain .edu, .net, .org, or .gov? (If you see a ~ in the URL, it may be a personal site, not an official site.)	**YES NO**	

Used with permission of Common Sense Education, https://www.commonsensemedia.org/educators

or not to trust a website. Then later, when we talk about reading for bias and perspective, I bring back Test before You Trust. The first question:

"Can you tell if the site is fact or opinion? (If the information is one-sided, or biased, you will have to go elsewhere to hear the other side of the issue)" (Common Sense Media, 2010).

Table 4.3 Test Before You Trust

Purpose of the site	Circle One	Add details to explain
1. Can you tell if the site is fact or opinion? (If the information seems one-sided, or biased, you will have to go elsewhere to hear the other side of the issue.)	**YES NO**	

Used with permission of Common Sense Education, https://www.commonsensemedia.org/educators

We then talk about why this might be the first question that you should ask yourself when evaluating a website. The discussion helps students see how important this question is. Additionally, they realize it's not enough to *notice* that a source is biased and contains only one side of the issue (which is a skill in and of itself). They also need to learn how to find a site that expresses the other side of the issue. Then maybe they won't need to walk away from the first site, as long as they're also reading the other perspective. Sometimes, sure, walking away will probably be the best bet, but wouldn't it be better if students were educated in being able to read both sides of an issue and then making their own judgment based on the evidence provided? Students at this age are individuating, but still feel very beholden to their parents and guardians' viewpoints; many will tell you what "their" political beliefs are, and it's a reflection of what they have heard in their homes. This is normal, and, in many respects, the point—many parents *want* their children to think similarly to themselves. However, we should give students the tools to decide things for themselves. They need to be able to read something and decide if the viewpoint is valid based on the evidence (or lack of evidence) presented. They need to be able to look at both sides of an issue, even when they don't agree with one side. Middle school history class is where students should start building and flexing those discerning muscles.

> We should give students the tools to decide things for themselves.... They need to be able to look at both sides of an issue, even when they don't agree with one side. Middle school history class is where students should start building and flexing those discerning muscles.

But How to Know if Something Is Biased?

Students need to be able to take something that has a particular perspective and pull it apart in order to describe what bias *can* look like. And really, all media present some kind of bias—and bias isn't necessarily bad, it just is. To that end, we look at both a video clip and a text, each with a particular perspective, and then talk about what to look for when you are trying to determine a source's perspective. I tell them that it's like riding a bicycle—once they figure out how to find perspective in what they read, it will be difficult to *not* do it.

Deconstructing a Video Clip

First we look at a clip. We watch the introduction of episode one of the History.com and Nutopia-produced "America: The Story of Us" (2010).

It has a sweeping intro, with majestic music and images underneath the voiceover:

> Adventurers sail across an ocean to start a new life; a nation is born.
> Which becomes the envy of the world.
> But in search of freedom, friends become foes.
> And these new Americans will wage a war against the world's greatest military power.
> We are pioneers . . . and trailblazers.
> We fight for freedom.
> We transform our dreams into the truth.
> Our struggles . . . will become a nation.

Usually, we watch it more than once. Students gather observations while watching. Then they answer the question: "What perspective does this source have?" Their observations are their evidence. This is when students discuss the soaring music, the words "freedom" and "truth," and the labels of pioneers and trailblazers. An adult would be able to come up with—even from this short clip—a nuanced explanation of the perspective of this particular introduction and why it's presented in this particular way. Some students may be able to do this as well—but for many of them, it's sufficient for them just to be able to say that based on the introduction, this particular video series likely has a positive view about America and thinks America is great.

This kind of analysis is often new to students. They are used to accepting anything presented in document style as fact, just as they do with textbooks. The idea that a documentary is presenting a particular perspective is new to them, and is something that needs to be explicitly addressed, again and again, over the course of the year. Soon, it will become second nature for students to wonder as they are watching something: What does this particular piece of media, text, etc., want me to think? But this can't happen until we give them practice with it.

Teaching this kind of analysis is key because it helps students transition into more "worldly" consumers of media. As middle schoolers in the digital age, they are constantly interacting with media—whether or not we their teachers are digital immigrants or digital natives ourselves, and whether or not we approve of their technology use. It is our job to provide students with the tools to deconstruct what they are exposed to, what they seek out, and what and where they look to for information.

Deconstructing Text

Although digital media is important and is not going anywhere any time soon, neither is text. Being able to read text will always be an important skill for students to acquire, so I help them along the way. To give them practice examining a text with pretty clear bias, I usually choose Howard Zinn's "Columbus and the Indians" from his *Young People's History of the United States* (2007). This particular excerpt describes Columbus as "hungry for money," and explains that he and his people "seized the Arawaks [native people] by force." There are more subtle hints in the text that lead a middle school reader toward Zinn's perspective, but there are also enough obvious indicators so that a spectrum of students can succeed with the activity and find evidence of Zinn's perspective of Columbus. Students become pretty familiar with Zinn by the end of the class (and Zinn is presented as a secondary source text in conjunction with a text of the opposite perspective, so that students are able to gather information and make their own informed evaluations of historical events). By the end of this activity, students can describe Zinn's general perspective. This is a helpful skill for them to have, not only when they are looking to examine perspective and bias, but also when they are trying to comprehend a text. Even texts like Zinn's that are written for young adults can be difficult to wade through at times. When students know what the basic tone and bent of a text is, they are better able to anticipate meaning, categorize information, and understand the text and its overall themes.

Once students are more adept at looking for clues to figure out a text's perspective, they become very attuned to it. When reading about the Election of 1860 in our *History Alive!* textbook, multiple students stopped the class when they ran into a sentence they felt expressed a particular perspective that was uncharacteristic of the usually even-toned book. Students took note of the sentence, which described the shelling of Fort Sumter: "A month later, hotheads in Charleston, South Carolina forced the issue" (Bower and Hart, 2002). Students expressed surprise that the textbook authors would use the word "hotheads," as it seems to be an inflammatory word that would align with the sympathies of the Northern cause. It wasn't that they necessarily agreed or disagreed with the interpretation, but that they noticed there *was* an interpretation. Because the book usually left out those kinds of adjectives, they were surprised. I am sure they would not have noticed that kind of thing earlier in the year, before we practiced deconstructing text to identify bias. They are now more aware when they are reading, and this then helps them to better examine an event and the sources that are explaining it.

Applying Analysis of Perspective

In order to give students practice looking at perspective, it isn't enough to just have them analyze primary and secondary historical sources—it's a good start but is not sufficient. Students also need to see that what they encounter each day in the news—whether it be in print, on the Internet, on an aggregate, on social media, or through YouTube—can be analyzed for perspective. Therefore, my monthly current events assignment (which is further explained in Chapter 6), is scaffolded so that students start analyzing the news for bias about three months into the year, and it also asks students to look for bias in day-to-day reporting. Students are tasked with finding a current event, and not only explaining it (to practice comprehension level/paraphrasing), but also analyzing it to see *how* it was reported. Students often struggle the first time they do this part of the current event assignment. They soon realize that in order to see an article's perspective, they may also have to go elsewhere to read another article (or perhaps multiple articles) on the same topic in order to get the full picture. Then they can go back and analyze the original article. That's why the comparison I-Chart exercise is such an important scaffolding tool. It opens up the idea that one historical event can have multiple interpretations or write-ups based on the historian's perspective. Although the I-Chart activity has students analyze dates that are, yes, years in the past, the current events assignment has students realize that contemporary and topical events have multiple perspectives too.

Once students can see the news in relation to other news, and text in relation to other text, they automatically begin seeking out more than one source whenever they need to find information. They search for differences, corroboration, and additional facts. With current events, students look at pieces that are being written now, about issues that are relevant now, and parsing them for their subtext. They ask themselves: What is the usual stance of the particular news site? This ability guides students with comprehension, in the same way that knowing Howard Zinn's usual take on things can help them orient themselves if the text is heady. They can look for adjectives, they can look at multiple sources, they can look to see how many quotations are being used, what evidence . . . but at this point, the skills of comprehension, analyzing bias and perspective, and evaluating the usefulness of a website are being triangulated by the student into one skill: to discern what the author really thinks about the subject or event that he or she is writing about.

Why All This Analysis in Middle School?

Middle school is a time when perspectives are challenged as students grow out of their younger selves and into more individuated versions of themselves. While this is happening, they are experiencing a maelstrom of emotions and social pressures that tug at their focus. They are also interacting with the world through ubiquitous and far-reaching technologies that allow them to see more than teenagers have ever been able to see in the past. They have more access—to each other and to the information held in the world's collective consciousness. So they need more tools. As teachers of this particular age range, we need to recognize that students need to be exactly taught how to navigate the Internet—not because they can't figure out how to use it—but because they are lacking the tools for *discernment*. This is not a rap on the middle schooler; it is simply the case that whether or not they realize it, they need help sometimes. They need help contextualizing, seeing the whole picture, and wading through the pool of sludge that can be found online. We can help them learn how to find the proverbial gold among the sludge.

> They need help contextualizing, seeing the whole picture, and wading through the pool of sludge that can be found online. We can help them learn how to find the proverbial gold among the sludge.

As middle school history teachers, we are in a prime position to teach these skills and provide opportunities for students to practice them in a purposeful and contextualized way. Middle school students are captivated by the idea that history isn't written in stone after all (except when it is—primary source hieroglyphics!). They love conflict and mystery— the stories of the Lost Settlers of Roanoke or of Amelia Earhart are the ones that captivate them. They wonder, "What happened? How is it that we *still* don't know?" And when the history is agreed upon (for the most part), they are engaged by the question of how we account for differences in secondary sources—even *primary* sources. They ask, "How does history get written?" Presenting history as fluid and open to interpretation gives students a window to become interested and involved. Connecting history to the present with current events—and examining contemporary events through perspective analysis—starts up critical thinking skills that will serve students well as they go through high school and even college. Historiography activates the part of the middle schooler that is genuinely interested, and gives them the understanding, the autonomy, and the skills to be able to join the conversation in a meaningful way.

Chapter 4 Self-Reflection

1. How do you introduce your students to the concept of historiography?
2. What ways do you teach your students to recognize and analyze perspective?
3. What tools and strategies do you use to help students differentiate between primary and secondary sources?
4. What strategies from this chapter are you thinking of utilizing? Explain.
5. What adjustments might you need to make for your own classroom and the needs of your students?

References

America: The Story of Us. A&E Networks, 2010.

Hart, Diane, Bert Bower, and Jim Lobdell. *History Alive! The United States through Industrialism.* Palo Alto, CA: Teachers' Curriculum Institute, 2002. Print.

Heafner, Tina, and Dixie Massey. *Strategic Reading in U.S. History.* Culver City, CA: Social Studies School Service, 2006. Print.

"Identifying High-Quality Sites (6–8)." Common Sense Media, 2010. Web. 20 Aug. 2015. <https://www.commonsensemedia.org/educators/lesson/identifying-high-quality-sites-6-8>.

Johnson, Paul. *A History of the American People.* New York, NY: HarperCollins, 1998. Print.

"Lunchroom Fight." *Stanford History Education Group.* N.p., n.d. Web. 21 Aug. 2015. <https://sheg.stanford.edu/lunchroom-fight>.

Zinn, Howard, with Rebecca Stefoff. *A Young People's History of the United States.* New York: Seven Stories, 2007. Print.

5

Writing in History

Making Arguments, Backing Them Up, and Citing Sources

How Writing Expectations Have Changed: A Personal Observation

I don't remember everything from middle school, but I do remember that we really didn't write much for middle school history. As I work on this chapter, I happen to be sitting with my husband and his sister, who attended the same middle school, and our small combined memory is in agreement: There was not a lot of writing in history class until high school. The main way we demonstrated understanding was by taking tests—fill in the blank, multiple choice, maybe short answer. Now, not only has writing instruction changed in the past couple decades so that writing *is* more of a focus in middle school history, but the quality of the writing and the kind of writing required of students has shifted as well. This important shift seems to be due to a myriad of things, including the increased use of technology, and the move away from knowledge gathering and memorization to critical thinking (a move that is likely a result of technology too). These changes, reflected in the Common Core State Standards, are becoming more and more prevalent in classrooms across the country.

These changes are important and reflect the changing nature—or what really ought to be the changing nature—of the social studies classroom. Before information was readily available on the Internet, students needed stronger memorization skills and a stronger context of common knowledge. It isn't that students don't need these things anymore, but rather these things are not nearly as important as before. If students can look something up, they don't need to memorize it. However, what they do need to learn, and what more progressive history classrooms and standards like the Common Core emphasize, is what to *do* with the knowledge they find. We need to teach students to become better at discerning what is valid information, to be able to compare sources, and to be able to evaluate information. If they aren't memorizing, they need to be working on different skills. And many of these skills are brought to bear in students' writing. Students are asked to evaluate, to write thesis-driven essays, and to use multiple sources to defend a point, rather than just compile and organize information about a topic from multiple sources.

> If students can look something up, they don't need to memorize it. However, what they do need to learn . . . is what to *do* with the knowledge they find. We need to teach students to become better at discerning what is valid information, to be able to compare sources, and to be able to evaluate information.

I *do* remember writing for eighth-grade English; it was an honors class, but the writing required was much more freeform than what is required of students now. I would imagine that this shift has to do with the advent of the personal computer for writing. When I was in middle and high school, it was not a given that students would have access to a computer. (It is not a given now either, due to serious issues with access. It is to be hoped that most schools have computers somewhere on campus that students can access for assignments at the very least.) Never was an assignment required to be typed until my senior year of high school. Now, computing allows for a more fluid editing and revising process; spell check and grammar check assume a more perfect copy; and typing allows for students to be able to write more and to be more precise, and for teachers to read the copy more easily than in the past. These small changes have led to teachers gradually increasing the level of writing required of middle school students. Middle school students are now expected to write longer work, better quality work, and more polished work than they were doing before computers became a "thing."

Writing in Middle School: What *Is* Developmentally Appropriate?

Good writing is such an important part of expressing oneself, both academically and in the world, that providing scaffolding and structure to help students be able to write stronger and clearer essays is, ultimately, a good thing. However, the only drawback is that at times, we are asking students to really do some mental footwork that they are just on the cusp of being *able* to do well. It's the kind of challenge that will hopefully be right in their Zone of Proximal Development (Vygotsky, 1978)—but for some it will be a little further out, and for some who haven't quite started to get into what Piaget called the Formal Operational Stage (Piaget and Inhelder, 1969) and are still working at a literal level, this will be a formidable challenge. As middle school teachers, we should remember that it's good to ask students to write critically; they *should* write. But it will be a challenge. Most aren't adept yet at thinking abstractly—they've just started—and while some take to it quickly, others will find it less comfortable.

> As middle school teachers, we should remember that it's good to ask students to write critically; they *should* write. But it will be a challenge. Most aren't adept yet at thinking abstractly—they've just started—and while some take to it quickly, others will find it less comfortable.

I have done a great deal of reflecting on what I am asking of students. *Is it too much? Is it enough? Too hard? Too easy?* I've had to adjust each year depending on my students; each group, each student comes in at a different place in terms of how ready they are to write and think critically. The changes I have made over time, and continue to make, reflect both the changes in our expectations for students as writers and my goal to meet them where they are and then raise those expectations.

The Evolution of Writing in My Class

Origins: My Assumptions

When I moved from teaching third grade to teaching eighth-grade U.S. History, I had certain assumptions about the writing level of my soon-to-be eighth graders. I had these assumptions because of the writing skills that I had been working on with my students, and because of the skills that I knew were being taught between third and eighth grades. When planning to teach that upcoming year of U.S. History, I identified writing as a skill I wanted to focus on and use as a means of assessment. Over the years, I have tried a great many strategies, assignments, and types of writing to meet my students' needs and improve their work. Some ideas have been more effective than others, and I always come back to the tried and true academic essay. But it's good to mix it up.

History Writing Assignment Staple: The Letter/Diary

The one kind of writing assignment/assessment I do remember having in history class as a kid is the staple "write a letter or diary entry as a particular historical figure" assignment. I've used this assignment myself, but as time has gone by, I've become a little more wary of using it on a regular basis. Although teaching letters and diary entries as primary sources is an incredible way to help students glean information from historical figures about motivations, details, and historical events, letter writing itself isn't currently an *en vogue* form of communication. While not everything a teacher does has to relate to the current lives of students, asking students to access their own creativity through letter writing is probably not going to be as effective as it was when I was going to school. Back then, kids did occasionally write letters themselves. Now, as teachers, we might have to show students *how* to write a letter in order to have them complete the assignment. Whereas the idea used to be that students already knew how to write a letter, and therefore, it is a strong writing assessment because it allows for creativity: the letter is written as if the student were "from the past," and it is in a format that they are familiar with, allowing for an increased personal connection. While I still like the idea of this assignment—mimicking what primary sources used to look like—it really doesn't connect to students' personal experiences anymore. They aren't intrinsically familiar with the format these days (maybe through email, but I find students rarely use email to communicate).

In fact, I used to assess my Revolutionary War unit with a letter. Students were to make up a character on the side of the rebelling colonists or on the side of the British and write a letter to a family member or friend explaining why the family member/friend should move to their side. Then, they were to pick two historical figures that we studied from that time period (e.g: Cornwallis, Colonel Tye, Joseph Brant, John Adams, Phillis Wheatley, Bishop Samuel Seabury, Abigail Adams etc.) who were on the same side—either the colonists or the British—and use each historical figure's opinions as evidence as to why the side they chose was "the correct one."

I did get some interesting responses—and some of the fake historical names that students created were really humorous—but as a writing assessment, it wasn't as good as it could be. Yes, it was similar to a persuasive essay, but after reading the letters, I always felt like the writing would be stronger if I had given a thesis-driven essay with a slightly different prompt. Aside from the humor, the letter format didn't add much of anything to the assignment. And the letter wasn't a format that students were all that familiar with writing outside of the classroom.

So if we want students to be able to connect to the past in writing, or if we want students to be able to show what they know through writing in a way that they are familiar with, what are we to do? Well, the answer changes every time a new form of technology comes out—especially when there are new ways for students to connect socially. When I first started teaching middle school, Facebook was still a thing, then Twitter, then Instagram, then Snapchat . . . students move platforms as soon as the platforms are "found out." But an interesting historical exercise would be to ask students to project a historical figure's thoughts, motivations, reactions, and opinions onto a current form of communication or social media. While it doesn't assess writing as well as a letter assignment, it at least can help students connect to content in a way that they are familiar with. Again, the letter/diary assignment isn't dead—but if your motivation for using it is for students to be able to connect with it, then some retooling will be necessary.

Trying Out Other Writing Options

While I've moved letter writing to the wayside, I am still always on the lookout for new ways for students to express themselves and their understanding through writing. This past year, I tried a version of critical incident writing to have students compare perspectives of Revolutionary War figures.

Assignment Snapshot: Critical Incident Writing

Critical Incident: The Signing of the Declaration of Independence

Background: When the Declaration of Independence (break-up letter with Britain) was signed (one of the things that happened to start the Revolutionary War), many people were for it: They thought that the colonies should rule themselves and that the British needed to get out of the colonies. Many were against it: They felt that the British were rightly in charge and that the revolt was misguided and may get those against Britain and the king hanged for treason.

    Freeze this incident in time

    Assignment: Using the information from the **whole unit**, and the interviews from the Walk and Talk, write **TWO** paragraphs from **two different historical characters' perspectives** of the critical incident (the signing of the Declaration). How did they feel about the signing and why? What did they think might happen? Which side would they be on? Why? Use historical context, but make logical inferences to fill in the narrative.

You may use first person, but keep all other writing conventions; make sure you proofread.

This assignment could be used for any critical incident in history. After all, a critical incident is an event that has significance for the person, and there are many historical events that were significant for a great many people. I tried this type of writing this year to mixed results. I think that if I had provided a stronger structure for writing up the critical incident itself, that might have been more helpful. As it was, it was a way to get students to move away from the letter writing, to think about multiple perspectives of an event, and to discuss the historical importance of a particular event. But this kind of writing assignment can be used for any critical event in history, like a moment during a war, the fall of a particular civilization, the invention of a new kind of technology . . . any event where there would be some kind of reflection that the historical figure could do: what the incident was, what his or her response was, what he or she would have done differently, what the effect of the incident was, and so on.

Looking back, I think that the critical incident writing needs to be much more than freezing an event in time. It should be the present self looking back on a critical incident, a significant moment. What I could have done was really flesh out each reflective section. Students could describe the incident and their reactions, the reactions of others, and the results. It would have been a fuller picture than what I had tried to do.

Why Critical Incident Writing in Middle School?

Middle school students both create and are subjected to a myriad of "critical incidents" during their time in middle school. The critical incident analysis model might serve more reflective purposes than just having students examine a historical event and its implications. If we could help students see the multiple uses of this model, students could apply it (with help) as a reflective tool to solve conflict in their own lives. The historical figure critical incident analysis writing can provide the structure and an example (either positive or negative) of people's reactions to significant events. Students have their own significant events each day, each week, so they could use some structure to analyze, reflect on, and imagine what they may have wanted to do differently.

While critical incident writing is something I've tried to varying success, the academic essay is a staple of my classroom and is something that I have worked hard to adjust over the years to better suit my students' abilities and needs. This particular kind of writing is often the most stressed in high school and college. Although I didn't get much of a chance to work on the academic essay as a middle schooler myself, I want my students to have familiarly and facility with it so that they are able to express themselves clearly and critically going forward.

To that end, I collaborated to create a five-paragraph essay scaffold that uses an outline and step-by-step process to guide students through opening their writing, crafting a thesis statement, transitioning, writing body paragraphs, backing up their assertions with evidence, and concluding. I feel strongly that for this age group, scaffolding is necessary—especially when we are asking them to go beyond the scope of a research paper and write an evaluative essay based on evidence.

Unit Snapshot: The Constitution

The first five-paragraph essay was the culmination of a thematic unit on the Constitution of the United States. It had students look at both the content of the Constitution and the various documents and ideas that influenced it and its creation. The influences that students examined included the Mayflower Compact (main contribution: consent of the governed), the Iroquois Confederacy (main contribution: united multiple factions under one centralized government/delegates), the Magna Carta (main contribution: limiting the power of the ruler), the English Bill of Rights (main contribution: giving delineated rights to the people), and Montesquieu's *Spirit of Laws* (main contribution: balance of power in three discrete branches of government).

The first iterations of this unit had students do some kind of constructivist activity to learn the influences, then read and engage with a text using a reading strategy like QAR or annotation, and then, finally, write a paragraph explaining how that particular influence actually influenced the Constitution itself. This paragraph called for a topic sentence, three supporting details drawn from the reading, and a conclusion. The idea was that each of these paragraphs would provide scaffolding in and of itself to be used, at least in spirit, for the final five-paragraph essay.

Now, looking back, it's interesting that so much tweaking has happened as a result of this initial five-paragraph writing assignment, but the tweaks were necessary. It's not because students couldn't hack it—they could—but it was truly challenging for them, and it was a lot of writing, especially since they had to churn out daily paragraphs in this format. Also, there wasn't any formal instruction built in about *how* to write these paragraphs—which in some ways was an important learning experience for students: They just had to go for it. My assumption had been that writing a strong paragraph, and by extension, a five-paragraph essay, was something that they had learned prior in history or language arts. However, the more time went on, the more it was clear that throwing students into the deep end was too emotionally taxing for them. They didn't seem to feel that they had the skills, and that is half the battle sometimes.

So, changes were made. Many changes were made.

The Process: Changes in Writing, Changes in Technology

One change I made was to do a writing workshop, beginning with some basic writing rules, such as limiting contractions and the first person, and *not* introducing a topic with the phrase "many ways," e.g. "The Iroquois Charter influenced the Constitution in many ways." (It's a pet peeve of mine; however, once students become proficient writers, they can break some of these rules.) This kind of explicit writing instruction helps middle school writers improve the structure and quality of their writing (Cihak and Castle, 2011).

This writing workshop then became, as much as possible, a one-to-one writing time where I would go around to students and help them craft their writing on the paragraphs—which, still, was very taxing, as they were often tasked to write one per day as the lessons kept on coming. As technology improved, this writing workshop morphed into a flipped-classroom style tutorial that asked students to create a checklist of things they should check their work for before having another person read it and before turning it in.

Then I started using Google Drive, and the collaboration that previously could only take place in the classroom became infinitely easier (though, in some ways more challenging for me as the teacher). Students would share a document through Google Drive, and I could offer suggestions and reminders, and ask for clarification about ideas. The one downside of Google Drive *is* the constant availability, which is also its best asset. Students will revise and edit, revise and edit, and if you have more than one student, it's a challenge to keep track of all of these revisions. And many students feel that with each revision, there needs to be validation from the teacher in order to move on. Some students will advocate and remind the teacher; others will wait passively. Regardless, it isn't the best system. I recommend setting clear due dates for drafts and then allowing one or two revisions on the drafts—or whatever limit you're comfortable with—instead of limitless revisions. The idea, though, is that the amount of work the teacher and student are putting in collaboratively on the front end is beneficial both in terms of the teacher's time later (in grading a finer-tuned piece of work) and also in terms of the students, who will ostensibly get something out of the process and benefit from a strong final draft. The process is also a way of encouraging student autonomy—if they don't submit a draft for revision, but then don't like their final grade, it can be a teachable moment for them. And that is what a great deal of middle school ends up being about: how to navigate the world and how to figure out what exactly one needs to do to succeed. This is not something that kids completely figure out in middle school—far from it—but there are so many opportunities to *practice*!

Challenge: Aligning Writing Goals

Another change I've experimented with recently, and am thinking about keeping around, is turning the final five-paragraph essay in the Constitution unit (the assignment that started it all) into a strong, evaluative paragraph instead. I have done this occasionally over the past two years, and it has worked out quite well. Why? Well, all of that individual paragraph writing isn't necessarily preparing students to write a strong five-paragraph essay, but it is preparing them to write a strong paragraph. So why not assess that? Additionally, I give the assignment at the beginning of the year, and due to scheduling, it is often a challenge to get all of the teaching in at the beginning of the year. Later, it is easier to scaffold these paragraphs into a five-paragraph essay about different content, and students keep their strong skills in paragraph writing throughout. That's not to say they don't struggle, but the quality of the five-paragraph essays that they do toward the middle and end of the year hasn't suffered just because they hadn't done a full essay earlier in the year. Additionally, introducing the "dreaded" five-paragraph essay later allows me time to introduce even scarier things, like citations and timed writings.

Adding in Citations . . . They Are Important

Once I had scaffolded my yearly assignments a bit more cleanly—though students still perceived the beginning of the year as a bit of a writing boot camp—I was able to focus more on citations and on other important aspects of writing. Citations were a surprising challenge for students. Five years ago, I didn't require students to cite sources directly if they didn't quote from the source. This was primarily because I explicitly asked them to only use sources provided by me in class. My reasoning? I really wanted to focus on this idea of creating a thesis and backing it up—I didn't want to add the extra variable of citations into the mix. I thought it would muddle the students' ability to grasp the writing skill we were working on. Perhaps this is true, but since I've added scaffolding by removing the five-paragraph essay at the beginning of the year, I think this concern has become less and less of an issue, and citations don't *have* to "come later." My realization that teaching citations doesn't have to wait came when I assigned an essay where there wasn't quite enough class material to use, and I let the students wander out into the vast wilderness of the Internet.

Here's what middle grade students totally get: If you use a quotation, you cite your source.

Here's what middle grade students struggle with: If you don't directly quote it and say it in your own words (paraphrasing—another challenging skill), then why would you need to cite it?

This difficulty took quite a bit of time, explanation, and just plain practice to overcome. And still, by the end of the year, there were a handful of students who still struggled with when to cite, who still felt that the only time it was necessary was with a quotation. What occurred to me was that it wasn't as important that students learn the specifics of proper citations with MLA, APA, Chicago, or whatnot, *nearly* as much as they learn that they *need* to cite when the ideas aren't theirs. And this is difficult for eighth graders, not to mention younger students. However, it's a very important skill, not only because citing sources is important—it is—but also because with the Internet, the risk of plagiarism is so much higher. Some schools (not mine) have Turnitin or other plagiarism checks. I still rely on Google if I need to, but I usually find that students who plagiarize don't realize that they are doing so (with a few exceptions, obviously). Often, the plagiarism is a result of a developmentally appropriate misunderstanding about what exactly are their words and what makes someone else's words and ideas *not* their own. This is the kind of thing that needs to be taught explicitly from the early grades and up; students might not get it right away, but they will eventually. Students need to be taught explicit tips for paraphrasing and for when to cite their sources—otherwise they'll be in hot water later. In fact, I've had conversations with students and their parents multiple times where we've discussed that middle school is a great time to make these mistakes. If you are going to plagiarize, do it in middle school. In high school and college, it is, as it should be, a much bigger deal. In middle school, it can be used as a difficult learning experience. A student might fail the assignment but will learn something about attribution that he or she isn't going to forget.

Often, the plagiarism is a result of a developmentally appropriate misunderstanding about what exactly are their words and what makes someone else's words and ideas *not* their own. This is the kind of thing that needs to be taught explicitly from the early grades and up.

Writing as a Tool to Assess Project-Based Learning

In an assignment that will be discussed further in the project-based learning chapter, I had my students do an entire unit around this inquiry question: "What caused the Civil War?" This was toward the end of the year, and by this time, students had worked on both citations and five-paragraph essays. One concern that some teachers have with project-based learning is that the outcomes are variable, depending on the individual student's output. Additionally, I had students in teams, and students were graded as a team. So, of course, I also wanted to be able to assess what they had learned in an individual way as well. So after each team finished their project that explained what caused the Civil War, I gave students two days to do a timed four-paragraph essay in class. Previously, I hadn't wanted to give timed writings, but I knew students would be expected to do them in high school, so I was motivated to try one. It was a challenge for the students. The prompt:

Write an in-class essay, 4 paragraphs, that answers the question "What caused the Civil War?"

You need to include:

- ◆ THESIS and intro (suggested prompt for thesis: _____ caused the Civil War, because . . .)
- ◆ Body Paragraph 1: Topic sentence/supporting details
- ◆ Body Paragraph 2: Topic sentence/supporting details
- ◆ Conclusion: So what?

> **Make sure to:**
>
> Cite any sources you use (remember both in-text and Works Cited
>   page)
> Proofread your work: no first person or contractions, and use
>   academic language
> Past tense for history
>
> You will be graded primarily on how well you use content and how
> well your supporting details support your thesis. You will also be
> graded on the strength of your writing.

As you can see, students are given reminders about writing tips, a sentence completion to help with their thesis, and a reminder of the elements of a four-paragraph essay. After two days, students turned in these essays, and the results were positive. Students, overall, used citations (not necessarily correctly) and were able to come up with a thesis and support it with evidence. While I had previously eschewed the idea of timed writing assignments, I was glad to have implemented one because it synthesized all of the writing elements that I had been working on with students all year. Additionally, it was a tool to assess whether the inquiry unit itself was successful. Again, as will be discussed in more detail in Chapter 8 of this book, this unit was inquiry/project based. Students were not looking at a one-size-fits-all set of events in a curriculum. They had to research on their own, and while I provided guideposts and monitoring, the lack of uniformity was a variable in whether the essays would turn out well. However, with the timed writing, I was able to see the facility with which students maneuvered facts, ideas, and large concepts that they had found in their research as evidence to back up their theses. To assess, I used, as I usually do, a rubric (see Table 5.1).

The content and the writing expectations are interwoven. The writing is a skill, scaffolded throughout the year, that, by this point, students will have some facility with. Once they do, they can focus more heavily on the content and can come up with abstract ways of explaining complicated historical events, such as the events that preceded the Civil War. The timed writing format, while stressful, allows me to see what my middle school

Table 5.1 Timed Writing Rubric

	4 Excellent	3 Meets Expectations	2 Approaching Expectations	1 Incomplete
Intro & Thesis	Clearly introduces topic of Civil War/causes, Thesis is clear, makes an argument, is not just a list of events	Introduces topic of Civil War/causes Thesis is present, not just a list of events	Intro is present, but unrelated to rest of paper Thesis is present, a list of events, unclear	Intro is not present or unclear Thesis is not present or unclear
Supporting 1	Uses relevant facts that support thesis	Uses mostly relevant facts to support thesis	Uses some facts to support thesis/thesis isn't fully supported	Uses little to no detail/facts
Supporting 2	Uses relevant facts that support thesis	Uses mostly relevant facts to support thesis	Uses some facts to support thesis/thesis isn't fully supported	Uses little to no detail/facts
Conclusion	Gets to a "so what" that connects to the thesis	Concludes and attempts a so what that connects to a thesis	Concludes, so what is unclear or not fully explained or not fully connected to thesis of paper	Does not conclude, does not attempt a so what, does not connect to thesis or rest of paper
Citations and Finishing	In-text and end-of-text citations are present and almost all are cited correctly Paper has been proofread Academic writing is strong	In-text and end-of-text citations are present and mostly cited correctly Paper has mostly been proofread Academic writing is present in places	In-text and end-of-text citations are mostly present and mostly cited correctly Paper has been minimally proofread Academic writing is infrequent; tone very colloquial	Very few to no citations (in text/end of text) Paper is in rough draft form Academic writing is rarely/not present.

students can do on their own (without help from parents, tutors, siblings, etc.) and gives them a taste of what many of their high schools will require from them—to be able to write in an organized way in a discrete amount of time.

Results: So What?

One of the hardest things for students to write is a conclusion. Sure, it'd be easy to just paraphrase the thesis and say it in different words, but what I ask students to do is to come up with a "So What?" This is very challenging for students. This is the part that is the least scaffolded; it's the part where we ask students to come up with why what they are writing matters, what the impact might be on history, and what the implications are for the present. It is the place in the essay that asks students to be the most developmentally mature that they can be, to think the most critically. Some can do it and some struggle. The conversations are always both difficult and fruitful.

Why Writing in Middle School? In Social Studies?

So what is the "So what?" for writing instruction in middle school? What's the point of asking students to write *more*, to write more critically, and to think more deeply if it is challenging and possibly a bit out of their reach developmentally? For one thing, students who gain practice writing like this should be more prepared for difficult and rigorous writing in high school and college.

Also, this kind of writing, while structured, allows students to be able to "get good" at writing before they are able to break the rules that we try to teach them at this age. And even if this kind of writing is hard for them, once they are able to come up with a strong argument that is well structured, they gain such a feeling of accomplishment that they *can* do it. Citations continue to be a challenge, but the importance of alerting students to the concept that others' ideas are property is an important one. This is also developmental to an extent. It's not necessarily appropriate for us to ask a student in elementary school to use citations—both the concept and the detail-oriented nature might put them off writing forever—but in middle school, well, that's the time to introduce this important principle of writing.

And as middle school teachers, we can provide the best of both worlds for our students—we can require of them a great deal but also provide the scaffolding that they need at this age to be able to succeed.

Moreover, with increased writing instruction, we can give students more of a platform than ever before to be able to write for an audience. We can help them create blogs on a number of student-specific blogging platforms, such as Edublogs (https://edublogs.org) or Kidblog (https://kidblog.org), so students can read each other's work more readily and share their writing with a larger audience—perhaps parents and other students in the school—or even a global audience, depending on what the school administration feels comfortable with.

Whether students are sharing with just their classmates or with a larger audience, this kind of thinking and analysis will serve them well as they negotiate the media that they encounter almost every waking moment of their lives. This kind of practice with analysis will allow them to be more discerning consumers of media and more astute thinkers in general. And these middle school students will be better prepared for a world where historical information (or any information, really) is readily available. Analytical writing in history class is one of the ways that students can tap into this idea of historiography and evaluation instead of just memorizing facts and taking a test on the information like I did in eighth-grade history class.

Chapter 5 Self-Reflection

1. Has the way writing is taught changed since you learned "how to write?" In what ways?
2. How have you changed the way you've taught writing over the years?
3. What place do you see writing in a history curriculum?
4. What strategies from this chapter are you thinking of utilizing?
5. What adjustments might you need to make for your own classroom and the needs of your students?

References

Cihak, David, and Kristin Castle. "Improving Expository Writing Skills with Explicit and Strategy Instructional Methods in Inclusive Middle School Classrooms." *International Journal of Special Education* 26.3 (2011): 9. Web. 15 July 2015.

Piaget, Jean, and Bärbel Inhelder. *The Psychology of the Child.* New York: Basic Books, 1969. Print.

Vygotsky, L. S. *Mind in Society: The Development of Higher Psychological Processes.* Cambridge: Harvard University Press, 1978. Print.

6

Relevance: Why Does This Matter to Me?

Social Context, Historical Legacy, and Current Events

To make history relevant—to make it matter to students—might be the whole point of history class. Every teacher wants his or her students to care about history. But it isn't an easy feat to make the subject area relevant to middle schoolers; these are students who need a real and deep reason to care. It can't be because of a standardized test, a grade, particular content, or a particular concept, and it can't just be because we, as adults, know this stuff is important and try to convince students that it really *is*. Students at this age need to make connections and seek honest meanings in order to internalize that history matters, and *should* matter to them.

> Students at this age need to make connections and seek honest meanings in order to internalize that history matters, and *should* matter to them.

There isn't one way to do this, of course. If there were a magic way to promote deep caring for content or for a discipline's importance, I am sure we history teachers would have heard of it already and would be using it. Instead, I've found that there are different tacks we as history teachers can take to make this subject resonate for students of this age. Some methods involve helping students better conceptualize the time and space of history, some involve helping students connect ideas from the past into their own terms and language, and some have students examine the reverberations of history into the present time. It's not a one-size-fits all situation, and it's an ongoing conversation. It is possibly harder to get a buy-in from middle schoolers than it is from kids at other grade bands. They aren't in elementary school anymore, so they have some autonomy as to whether they want to buy in or not, and they aren't in high school, where grades are often a strong motivating factor. We have to *prove* to middle schoolers that they should care. We know we need to make history relevant for our middle school students, and we are all working on *how* to do it.

Contextualizing in Time and Place

As I've mentioned earlier in the book, one of the things to remember when teaching middle school students is that not all of them have moved out of what Piaget has deemed Concrete Operations and into Formal Operations (Piaget and Inhelder, 1969). Many students will still be rather literal—more and more so, the younger they are. So it is important not to take anything for granted. Students may have a conception of the past and the present, but it might be rudimentary at best. Students need nuance, shading, and help to be able to understand the time period in history (and region) you might be examining. It's not that they need you to just tell them over and over how many years ago it was, etc., but that they need some tools to help them contextualize, in time and place, both the present and the historical content they are examining. For example, sometimes when we talk about George Washington, I will have students try to calculate how many great-grandparents are between their time and Washington's time. This helps them put an abstract concept into more quantifiable terms. Tricks like this enable students to connect to the past temporally—which they need to do, or else the topic will feel even further removed than it has to.

Teaching with Themes

Counterintuitively, one way to help students contextualize is by having them study themes rather than discrete time periods. For example, if you choose to arrange your units thematically, you could have a unit on Religion, or Inventions, or the like. These could be spread out content-wise among the civilizations, time periods, or places that the students engage with throughout the year. So instead of just going with what happened first, students will look deeply into a concept over time, over place, sometimes even over civilizations. The drawback to this method is that, while it can help students recognize larger cohesive themes over different places, times, and cultures, it can confuse matters in terms of the linear-ness of history.

Timelines

One way to ease students' confusion, whether you chose to teach thematically or chronologically, is to provide timelines. Since I teach U.S. history, most of the events and concepts on my timeline are from or related to U.S. history. I have it organized so that everything of note that we study during the year is placed on the timeline in three discrete categories that are color-coded and stacked: documents/laws, events (wars), and land acquisitions. Land acquisitions are in red on the lowest level of the timeline; documents/laws (anything written) are in the middle in purple; and wars or events are on the top in green. In this way, students can see the key laws that were enacted, the land acquisitions, and the major events, all at the same time (see Figure 6.1). For example,

Figure 6.1 U.S. History Timeline

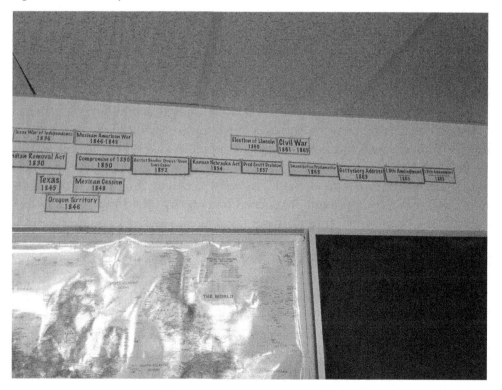

the Mexican-American War is visually above the acquisition of the Mexican Cession at the bottom and, shortly thereafter, in the middle the Compromise of 1850. Students can then see the catalyzing effect that the Mexican-American War and the subsequent acquisition of California, Nevada, Utah, and New Mexico had on the politics of the country, leading up to the Civil War.

You may want to organize your timeline in a different fashion, especially if you are dealing with much larger swaths of history (for example, if you teach Ancient Civ. or World Civ.). But think about three (or more) categories that you can stack in such a way that students see the interplay between chronological events. For example, in a World History class, the stacks might work best as different civilizations—that way students can see how they interact linearly. But, again, students need to be able to *see* when past events happened in relation to other events. Time is not the easiest concept to grasp, and we do our students a disservice if we don't provide them with some scaffolding to help them along the way.

> Students need to be able to *see* when past events happened in relation to other events. Time is not the easiest concept to grasp, and we do our students a disservice if we don't provide them with some scaffolding to help them along the way.

Maps

History teachers have always put an important emphasis on teaching students map skills and how to locate where in the world (according to a map) a place is/was or an event is happening/happened.

Many maps that are being made and used today in schools aren't usually drawn in correct proportions. Africa is much bigger than it is usually drawn, and the United States and Europe are both smaller. This difference can affect the way students see themselves and others in the world, and these changes represent worldviews—they weren't done by accident. For years (until I got an IdeaPaint Wall and ran out of space), I had an "upside-down" map of the world in my classroom. Students forget that since Earth is a sphere rotating in space, there *is* no up or down, and the top of the world is only the top if it's drawn like that. Not only does this kind of map shake students out of their complacency and help them see the world differently, but it also helps them build upon those critical thinking skills of Piaget's formal operations. Students in middle school are used to thinking that what they see in a text or on a map is correct and that it is *the* way to think about things. Showing students that the directionality of a map, like other things, is a construct and a historical habit can lead to greater conversations about *why* maps might always be drawn in that particular way and can lead students to examine other assumptions that they may hold.

In addition to having students analyze these types of maps, we can also have them use a much newer and different tool—Google Earth. Google Earth somewhat removes the perspective of directionality. If your school has access to technology, it can be an amazing way for students to see not just where in the world something is, but also what it might have looked like in the past, and how far away it is from major waterways, oceans, other countries, etc. In the study of ancient civilizations, there is a great deal of interconnectivity, and with Google Earth, students can move from place to place, simulating the physical trajectory of ideas throughout space and time.

Students can incorporate Google Earth into their projects and presentations to show classmates where they are talking about, and teachers can quickly pull it up during a lesson in order to clarify where a place is in relation to other areas.

When my students study the lost colony of Roanoke at the beginning of each year, they are always excited to pull up Google Earth, and they pretend to search for clues and the mysterious island of Croatoan.

Physical maps are improving—hopefully places are also being represented more accurately in proportion to each other, but technology, too, has come a long way in helping students use maps to ground themselves in space and time. And when students feel like they understand where and when a place was in space and time, it is so much easier for them to care about what is being taught Visually, maps make such a difference: They enable students to make connections they wouldn't have been able to otherwise. Just being able to show students in "street view" what things look like in the world, both today and in the past, goes a long way to helping them connect to history.

> But technology, too, has come a long way in helping students use maps to ground themselves in space and time. And when students feel like they understand where and when a place was in space and time, it is so much easier for them to care about what is being taught.

Making History Relevant

Students want to know: Why does history matter? And why does it matter to *me*, now, as a middle schooler? They want to see in what ways this study of "stuff that happened way in the past" can connect to their lives now. It's like a dare, really. In the worst case scenario, middle school students are sitting in class waiting for you to prove to them that history *actually* matters. (They're probably doing something similar in all their classes, so history doesn't have to take it personally.) Let's take the dare and work to bring the past into the present. One way I do this is by bringing in music that is thematically relevant and that students can connect with.

Using Music in the Classroom

Music, contemporary or otherwise, can be an important tool to hook students into making connections with content. In my class, music has often been the way that students first approach a particular subject. For example, as mentioned earlier, when we do a unit on the drafting of the Constitution, we begin with the idea that there are multiple views of America. We look at those views through the lenses of Charlie Daniel's Band and Tupac. Students analyze the lyrics of two songs and compare them: What is the tone and content of each? How do they feel about America? Why? What evidence (song lyrics) do they cite as the reason? Each year it surprises me how often students will go back to some of the concepts (especially in Tupac's "Changes") to explain a point that they have, or to compare contemporary issues with problems that have their historical roots in the past. The songs help students see that while the format of expression may change, some of the themes stay the same.

KRS-One's "The Sound of the Police" is another song that helps students to connect the present with the past. The perspective of the song is that both overseers during the time of slavery and police officers are similar/the same. Whether or not one agrees with the group's comparison, it is their perspective. Students delve into the way that the group uses images of slavery to make their point about the way African Americans are treated in this country. Students can then look more closely at why the history of this country matters today, and why the perspectives of people of color might be different from the perspectives of people who have grown up with cultural privilege. Students will see their own views reflected in the contemporary social commentary of rappers and other artists.

Or perhaps they will be sparked and inspired by history through a soundtrack like Lin-Manuel Miranda's *Hamilton: An American Musical*, which incorporates people of color into the narrative of the founders and the American War of Independence. Miranda's narrative, which is based on Ron Chernow's book *Alexander Hamilton*, repaints Alexander Hamilton's narrative as an immigrant who has succeeded beyond measure to shape the future of his adopted country. These kinds of things will likely speak to the students, their experiences, and their hearts more than a teacher's or a text-book's words.

Of course, this is not to say students have to listen to current music. It can also be powerful for them to listen to music from a particular period in history to get a better understanding of that time. Music can be the common medium to help students connect to novel or challenging times and themes, rather than the themes themselves being the common thread.

For example, when we study the Civil War, I like to use music written in that era to help students see what was happening in the hearts and minds of those involved in the war. The album *Divided & United: The Songs of the Civil War* is a good collection of Civil War-era songs (sung by contemporary artists); students can analyze these songs and parse them for context and content, and get a clearer picture of the world during the war. The song "Kingdom Come," which was typically sung by white minstrel players, is an interesting take on whites' perspective of slaves on a plantation, while the plaintive "Johnny Has Gone for a Soldier" really takes the sadness and fear of war and makes it easier to empathize with. Songs that were written in the time period can help students see what was important to people at the time. It can also help them see what would later be seen as the most important cause from a time period—for example, the infamous "John Brown's Body" was an anthem for the Northern cause.

In the same way, music and musical instruments from different time periods in history—such as the Renaissance or Chinese opera music—can help students better understand the depth and breadth of the culture and the time period they are studying. Students might not be able to relate to the ideas and concepts of that time period, but they can certainly relate to the need to create and listen to music.

Writing Parodies

Because music has always been such an important way for me to get across big ideas or solidify important points during my units, I was excited when I ran across Mr. Betts's parody of "What Does the Fox Say?" entitled "What Does John Locke Say?" (https://www.youtube.com/watch?v=kItXvJLnTtk). I planned to use it to kick off my comparison of Locke and Jefferson's ideas. It's the kind of activity that gets students grounded in a subject, gets them hooked and excited—and possibly most important for middle schoolers— gets them thinking that talking about John Locke *might* be cool (especially if the parody is done well, as Mr. Betts's is).

Watching his parody, though, made me wonder: Would the kids be even more connected if they wrote their own parody songs? Coming up with a really good parody actually requires a number of skills, the most important being the ability to synthesize and connect content to the trappings of the present. So I created a project in which students could select a content area of their choice, and a song that was appropriate for school, and then somehow combine these things to create something new.

To choose content, students had to discuss and go over everything we'd studied so far. Just that conversation alone required them to put together all the disparate pieces of what they'd learned in the year so far in order to decide what content they would focus on. This led to discussions heavy with review and discernment. Then students began gathering the most important points to be able to synthesize content into an actual parody song. These songs—no matter when in the year the students do them and how much material they have to work with—are always impressively astute in terms of the content chosen, and in terms of the song chosen as a vehicle to express that content.

Why a parody? At first glance, it would seem like simply a way of pandering to the middle school student's preferred mode of cultural expression. However, it is much more than that. True, students might be hooked into the idea that they are getting to use their own music to explain and express historical contexts, but they soon realize that it is a much more challenging job than they'd thought. They will persevere, though, because they are crafting something that has value to them, and that brings the concepts they are studying into their own lives, at least in a small way, and makes them memorable.

Bringing Historiography into the Present

As I mentioned when talking about primary and secondary sources in Chapter 4, one of the activities I have students engage in is the creation of a secondary source narrative from primary source documents. This activity does more, though, than just teach students the difference between a primary source document and a secondary source. It is also a way to have students understand that historiography is an ongoing process and a process that they themselves can be part of.

Assignment Snapshot: Secondary Source Narrative

Your assignment:

Write a secondary source narrative, like a biography, from the information about the primary source documents that you have collected.

Make sure you write it in chronological order.

If at any point you get stuck, watch the Secondary Source Narrative video from the "Now What" slide.

For this activity, I give students a ton of primary source documents from my life: my birth certificate (slightly redacted), my sons' ultrasounds and birth announcements, programs from plays, pictures, letters from middle school, wedding invitations, certificates from kindergarten, diplomas, and assorted odds and ends from my life that could prove interesting "evidence" for these students to collect. I don't tell them that these are primary source documents from my life, per se, only that they are all primary source documents from one person's life and it is their job to piece together the evidence in these primary source documents in order to create a secondary source narrative. The process of collecting evidence takes a few days. Students work together in collaborative teams (though everyone writes for him or herself) piecing through the evidence bit by bit, and using the notes protocol (see Chapter 2), to draw conclusions about how the evidence fits together to create a picture of a person.

In this particular assignment, students are challenged by the fact that my name is quite different in some places (my given name is Jacqueline and is on most official documents). Given the iterations of my nickname, full name, and married name, students need to really piece things together and use the power of deduction, logic, and group thinking to figure out what might have happened that would result in some of these name differences.

Students also struggle in this activity with the scope of the inferences they make. While they are meant to gather evidence and then draw conclusions from the evidence, they sometimes take the evidence too far. For example, when looking at a picture of a graduation, they will assume it is a particular graduation (college or high school), when the evidence cannot

Figure 6.2 Secondary Source Narrative Instructions

Gathering clues in a Gallery Walk:

In this class, we are going to be detectives, we are going learn about people and events in history through clues. But, just like detectives have rules they have to follow, you also have to follow certain **rules**.

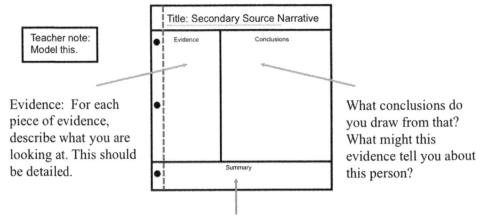

Evidence: For each piece of evidence, describe what you are looking at. This should be detailed.

What conclusions do you draw from that? What might this evidence tell you about this person?

Summary: From the evidence, piece together a narrative (story). Whose narrative is this? What have you learned about this person? Tell their life story BASED ON THE EVIDENCE YOU FOUND.

tell them that specifically. Or they will assume that a person next to me in a picture is a sibling, etc. These assumptions, mistakes, are really learning experiences in this assignment.

Once students gather all of the information they can, they sort it in chronological order. Last year, some of the students began crowdsourcing a timeline on the IdeaPaint Wall, which was a great way for them to begin the challenging work of putting all of the information in order.

And finally, when students sit down on their own to write the secondary source narrative, after days of having sifted through primary source documents, they realize what holes they might have in the narrative. Some feel compelled to add in "color" in the form of evaluative adjectives or embellish from the evidence to create narratives that aren't grounded in the documents themselves. These are inevitable and a good learning experience.

Once students have finished, they compare their narratives and are always confused as to how to account for the differences between each person's telling of the life story. They were looking at all the same primary source documents, so why are there differences?

From there, we talk about being careful in historical interpretation. We discuss that some of the incorrect information comes from their good intention of wanting to create a fuller narrative, but that ultimately, some of the information given in the secondary source narratives is the author's fabrications. Besides making inferences that go too far, what accounts for the difference? One factor is that students do not always label the same source documents as the most and least important. Each student (like each historian) brings unique experiences and perspectives to the interpretation of history that can't be disregarded just because students are engaged in the same task as everyone else. We bring ourselves to our interpretation, just like historians do.

Sure, students can learn a great deal about the difference between primary and secondary source narratives from this activity, but they also learn that the process of interpreting history is messy, that it requires a great deal of close reading, that it reflects the experiences of the interpreter, and that it can happen right now. Students often feel like historical interpretation is over—that historiography, like the history itself, happened in the past and doesn't have anything to do with them. By having students engage in historiography work themselves, they see that they can be a part of the process and engage in the work of historians, too.

> Students often feel like historical interpretation is over—that historiography, like the history itself, happened in the past and doesn't have anything to do with them. By having students engage in historiography work themselves, they see that they can be a part of the process and engage in the work of historians, too.

My first class that I worked on this assignment with came up with a group definition of what history is after completing this process: **"History is a narrative of a series of events, that is pieced together from evidence and the opinions of interpreters."**

When students count themselves as one of those interpreters of history, they have come a step closer to seeing history in the present. Whether the content in the class is Ancient Civilization, World History, or U.S. History, this beginning exercise in historiography and interpretation can bring students into the process in a meaningful way.

Making it Matter

Rights: Why Does Government Matter?

As teachers, we know history class has relevance to the present. But, again, you can't just tell this to a student and expect him or her to tacitly agree. For example, government, whether it is American, Roman or Greek, Chinese, monarchic, democratic, democratic-republican, matters. And it really matters to historical interpretation, and it really, really matters to know about the government you currently live in. But again, you can't tell that to students—they don't care until they have to, or until they somehow *see* or feel or experience that it is important.

My students study and research different government types (see Chapter 8), and this leads to an in-depth study of the U.S. Constitution. The part of the Constitution that students naturally gravitate toward is the Bill of Rights, written about ten years after the text of the Constitution. The Bill of Rights delineates what rights that people in the United States are entitled to; these rights are, depending on which one, both specific and general, and have guided constitutional law and the law of the United States since their inception. Students don't always care about the Bill of Rights, but they do like that it is in a list of ten.

While they might not currently be in a position to care about these rights, they may need to care at some point. Students should know what their rights are, otherwise they won't know if their rights are being violated. Students should know that if they were ever in the position to be arrested (and hope against hope they wouldn't ever be), they should know they have a right to a lawyer, the right to not pay bail or fines that are too high, the right to a speedy trial, and the right to not incriminate oneself. Students should know what free speech and the First Amendment entail. Wherever they live, it is our hope as teachers that they will know what their rights protect and what they don't. However, just because we want them to know how important and meaningful these rights are, doesn't mean that students will feel the same way. (And we don't want them to *really* feel it and be in a bad situation where they need to call upon their rights, of course.) However, we want them to feel the *importance*. We can have students look at the world around them, choose something they feel violates an amendment, and write a message, tweet, or email to a congressperson explaining what they think needs to change and why. They can look at Supreme Court cases and decide if the decisions violate or protect constitutional rights.

In order to examine the intricacies of governing, students can create their own governments—based on a current or past model, in this or another country or civilization—and try to govern based on the rules of that government. In a simulation atmosphere, some students can be the governing bodies and others can be those who are governed. They can experience what it's like to have particular rights, or lack thereof, and they can see in what instances rights might be really helpful to have, whether it's habeas corpus, or the right to assemble peaceably. After simulating a real government, students can work in teams or as a class to create what they think the ideal government should be, how much power the government should have, and what rights people should have.

Once they've experienced the simulation, they will be much more likely to see how the rights that they have here in this country can impact their real, actual, middle school lives.

Difficult Subjects: Slavery, Genocide, and Colonialism

When teaching any subject, whether it is World History, Ancient Civilizations, Western Civilizations, or U.S. History, there are difficult parts of the past that we may feel compelled to gloss over. It is easier that way: We can avoid having hard conversations about material that might be uncomfortable and that might make the teacher or the students feel a collective guilt about something, and we can avoid questions about good and evil or possibly even theology. However, it would be a mistake to pretend like these difficult things didn't happen. Why? Well, one reason is that we don't want those who are ignorant of history to be doomed to repeat it, but there's more than that. It is also that students can't really understand the world that they're living in unless they look at the difficult past that people have endured to see why things are the way they are.

> Students can't really understand the world that they're living in unless they look at the difficult past that people have endured to see why things are the way they are.

For example, in U.S. History class, we look closely at the history of slavery, but also at how the legacy of slavery affects the country and cultural relations today. This can bleed into current events, and it should. Students can look closely at how slavery—and then the promises, successes, and failures of Reconstruction, and then segregation and housing restrictions—limited the rights and shaped the experiences of African Americans in this country. Last year, after learning about Reconstruction, students in my class read Ta-Nehisi Coates's article "The Case for Reparations" (http://www.theatlantic.com/magazine/archive/2014/06/the-case-for-reparations/361631/), and debated whether and how the country could make reparations for families who have been, over the many years of this country, affected by the legacy of slavery.

Students need to have these conversations, and they need to be taken seriously. Simulations are not the place to examine these difficult issues. While there has been a push to include gaming in the classroom, we should be careful of using games for tough topics. For example, a current game out of Denmark called "Slave Tetris," where the gamer is meant to stack slaves in configurations into a slave ship, is perhaps the worst way to discuss the horrors of the Middle Passage and the Triangular Trade with students.

In World History, students need to learn about the Holocaust in order to understand the experience of Jews in Europe, America, Israel, and really everywhere. Is this a difficult conversation? For sure, but it is imperative to have. Currently the last generation of survivors (those who were very young during the Holocaust) are telling their stories and the stories of their families and parents. For this particular historical event, the stories are the most important way to help students see the relevance of the event, even if they haven't had a personal connection to either the Holocaust or to Judaism. These stories can be difficult to hear but are the last vestiges of this historical event; they are primary source texts for students to delve into. The USC Shoah Foundation (http://sfi.usc.edu) archives the stories of survivors, and this can be a good resource if you are looking for first-person testimony of this or other genocides in the world. Additionally, Facing History and Ourselves (https://www.facinghistory.org) has meaningful programs to help to contextualize and make meaning from some of history's most difficult chapters, as well to help make the lessons of history matter for students today.

Colonialism is another important topic to discuss. We tend to look at it as a fact of history, instead of as a system that created a great deal of suffering in certain regions of the world, specifically in Africa. For example, the Rwandan Genocide of 1994 can be traced to the colonial rule of both the Germans and the Belgians. When students are studying U.S. History, they should know that colonialism was happening everywhere, not just in the United States. And when students are studying the Roman Empire, or the

Ottoman Empire, they can trace some of today's international tensions back to those times.

There isn't a right way to have these difficult conversations, besides making sure we treat these subjects with respect and care. Despite the challenges of raising these issues, we can't avoid doing so. Students need to see that the problems of the world they live in were not built in a vacuum but are rather vestiges and legacies of the past.

Current Events: Who Cares Right Now?

And finally, one of the hardest, but most important ways to make history relevant to students is to have them look hard at what is happening in the world right now and connect these ideas to both the content and skills that are being worked on in class.

My students do a current events project each month. I try to have students bring parents, siblings, grandparents, aunts, uncles, guardians, into the conversation in a meaningful way so that the adults in each student's life can see the work that the student is able to do, and so that the student can discuss complicated topics with others, rather than just on their own.

This assignment is scaffolded. First, students find an article, give their opinion, and discuss another person's opinion. At this point, students are just finding a particular current event and evaluating it to their best ability in conversation with an adult.

Your Assignment: Take One

Choose an article about a current event that relates to the United States. Links to credible news sources can be found on the current events page.

Write one paragraph describing your family member's view about the topic.

Write one paragraph describing your own views about the topic and why you think that way.

◆ Make sure to include the name of the article and its source in your title and include a link to the article that you used.

The next time that they do the assignment, I make it more challenging: They have to look at the way in which the article was reported. To do this, they will often have to look at more than one article to get the full picture. This requires students to pick articles that have a bit more substance. Then they continue to evaluate the event and discuss it with an adult.

Your Assignment: Take Two

Choose an article about a current event. Links to credible news sources can be found on the current events page. Make sure to:

- Include the name of the article in your title
- Include the name of your source in your title
- Include a link to the article you used.

Write one paragraph explaining the event. **Identify the bias/perspective of your source.**

- Write one paragraph describing your family member's view about the topic, **and on the way in which it was reported.**
- Write one paragraph describing your own views about the topic and why you think that way. Also, **describe what you think about the way in which it was reported.**

Finally, I have students do all of the above, but then also tie the current event into one of our course themes:

- **The idea of America has been associated with the ideals of freedom, equality, and opportunity; the ideals do not always reflect reality.**
- **The United States functions by maintaining a balance between opposing groups/powers.**
- **The use, disuse, and misuse of new technologies are crucial in shaping the events in a country's history.**

This helps students see that current events are becoming part of their own history, and that current events tie to these themes that we have been examining throughout the year. No matter how you organize your history curriculum (by themes, standards, etc.), you can have students tie current events to something they're studying so they can make these connections.

Your Assignment: Take Three

Choose an article about a current event. Links to credible news sources can be found on the current events page. Make sure to:

◆ Include the name of the article in your title
◆ Include the name of your source in your title
◆ Include a link to the article you used.

Write one paragraph explaining the event. Identify the perspective of your source.

Write one paragraph describing your family member's view about the topic, and on the way in which it was reported.

Write one paragraph describing your own views about the topic and why you think that way. Also, describe what you think about the way in which it was reported.

Finally, write one paragraph that connects this event to one of the three themes of our U.S. History class (these can be found on our U.S. History Main Page).

Making History Matter in Middle School

Middle school students need to be reeled in and made to care about the content, but sometimes they are hard to hook. How do we get them to care? Again, there isn't just one way, but having them connect the past to the present is often the best way to do it. Current events occasionally do strike a chord in middle school students, so discussing them is paramount—especially if it's something they're interested in. If it's difficult to connect a current event to the content you're covering in class, try to connect it to a concept they've studied previously, or even better, have the *students* try to connect it. And don't forget scaffolding and support; middle school students need help to be able to contextualize history. Timelines and maps help, but for the "making them care" part, you have to get students to feel something. Music is a great way to help students empathize with how historical figures might have felt about things, or how the events of history have shaped the world today. And the study of people, which I will talk about in the next chapter, is also a really important way to help students connect to the "who-ness" of history.

Chapter 6 Self-Reflection

1. How do you make history relevant to your students?
2. In what ways do you bring current events into your classroom?
3. What kinds of difficult conversations have you had in your history classroom? What tools have you used to help facilitate those conversations?
4. What strategies from this chapter are you thinking of utilizing?
5. What adjustments might you need to make for your own classroom and the needs of your students?

Reference

Piaget, Jean, and Bärbel Inhelder. *The Psychology of the Child*. New York: Basic Books, 1969. Print.

7

Engagement

Historical Figures, Field Trips, and Games

How Do We Engage Students in the Study of History?

In history classes of yore (or at least in *my* own eighth-grade history class), it was standard to assume students were engaged in a task if they were quietly taking notes. If they made any kind of noise, they were considered to be off task. Thankfully, this isn't the case any longer. But student engagement is still a tricky business. If students are engaged, then they are busy, they are occupied, and they are working. But does this mean that they have to be happy? Having fun?

I would argue that history cannot always be fun, but it can almost always be engaging. Students aren't always readily engaged by being lectured to (unless the speaker is incredibly charismatic and interesting). They can be engaged in writing or reading and annotating—and not necessarily have a ton of fun doing it—but it *will* activate their brains and make them work. The more challenging activities *will* engage them. Projects will engage students, because they will have to use so many different skills autonomously (more about that in the Chapter 8), and those can be both engaging *and* rigorous. But there is something to be said for activities that can engage and entertain, too . . . So then how do we best engage students and have them activated, working, and truly immersed in what they are doing?

It seems that usually, students are most engaged when they are experiencing their own learning. This kind of learning reaches a pinnacle in well-crafted project-based learning experiences, but can also be seen in field trips, simulations, games, and intense research into historical figures.

And middle schoolers need to be engaged in class because they are otherwise embroiled in their own, more engaging narratives. Better that they look at historical drama; it can give them needed perspectives, and it can temporarily pull them from themselves and the siren song of their social community to the larger sphere of historical consciousness.

Historical Figures

I once heard someone say that students can't really connect to history unless they connect to the people of history. While I don't know if I agree with the totality of that statement, I do believe that students need to connect to the human-ness of historical figures to truly understand their motivations, their lives, and the context of the history that surrounded them.

> Students need to connect to the human-ness of historical figures to truly understand their motivations, their lives, and the context of the history that surrounded them.

Body Bios

The main vehicle that my students use to uncover information about historical figures is the body biography (or body bio for short). When I taught third grade, I used a version of this that might be more suitable for younger middle schoolers (see Figure 7.1).

The verbs, of course, can vary depending on the historical figure and on what you want the students to research and ultimately do with the body bio. But the idea is that students' research goes much further than simply finding out when and where the person lived and died and who they were married to, etc. With this format, the students must look more deeply into motivation, feeling, impact, and creation.

Similarly, the body bio I use with my older middle school students looks deceptively easy, but it requires a great deal of critical thinking (see Figure 7.2).

Because it does look deceptively simple, some of my students shrug off the modeling and explanation I provide, only to be caught off guard when the assignment turns out to be much more challenging than they anticipated.

As a result, I created a flipped video that students can watch, either at home or in class, that will help guide them through steps that they might

Figure 7.1 Simple Body Bio

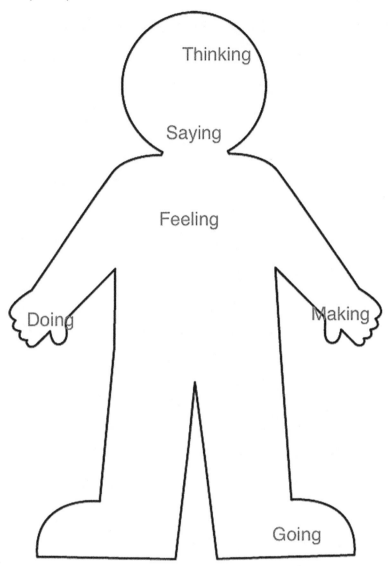

have missed or thought were so "easy" that they didn't need to pay attention. I find that the main difficulty with the body bio comes in the classification aspect—I've had students come to me and say that that part is so challenging, can they just make a list of the important events in this historical figure's life? The answer I give is that the challenging part is really

Figure 7.2 Complex Body Bio

one of the most important parts of the assignment—though obviously, if it is too challenging, I support students so that it isn't out of their Zone of Proximal Development (Vygotsky, 1978). The video is one element of support (they can pause it as needed), and there is also an example that students can watch over and over if need be. I can also help by pointing students in the right direction; often when they get stuck, it's because they are looking at the minutiae of the historical figure's life and need to be pointed to the right area of the biography.

The evaluation and research parts are also challenging. To complete this particular body bio, student must look up influences (those are the arrows at the top), thoughts (the thought bubble), feelings (the heart), good things/events (happy face), and bad things/events (sad face) (see Figure 7.3).

While this might sound straightforward—and, like I mentioned, students think so at first—it's tougher than it looks because most historical texts are not written in these particular categories, so students have to work like detectives, not only to find the information that is in the text but also to infer from the information the value of the historical figure. They also have to evaluate events from their own current perspective.

This body bio, or the simpler version, can be used for any social studies class (and could be used for other disciplines as well), but I've most often

Figure 7.3 Body Bio Explanation

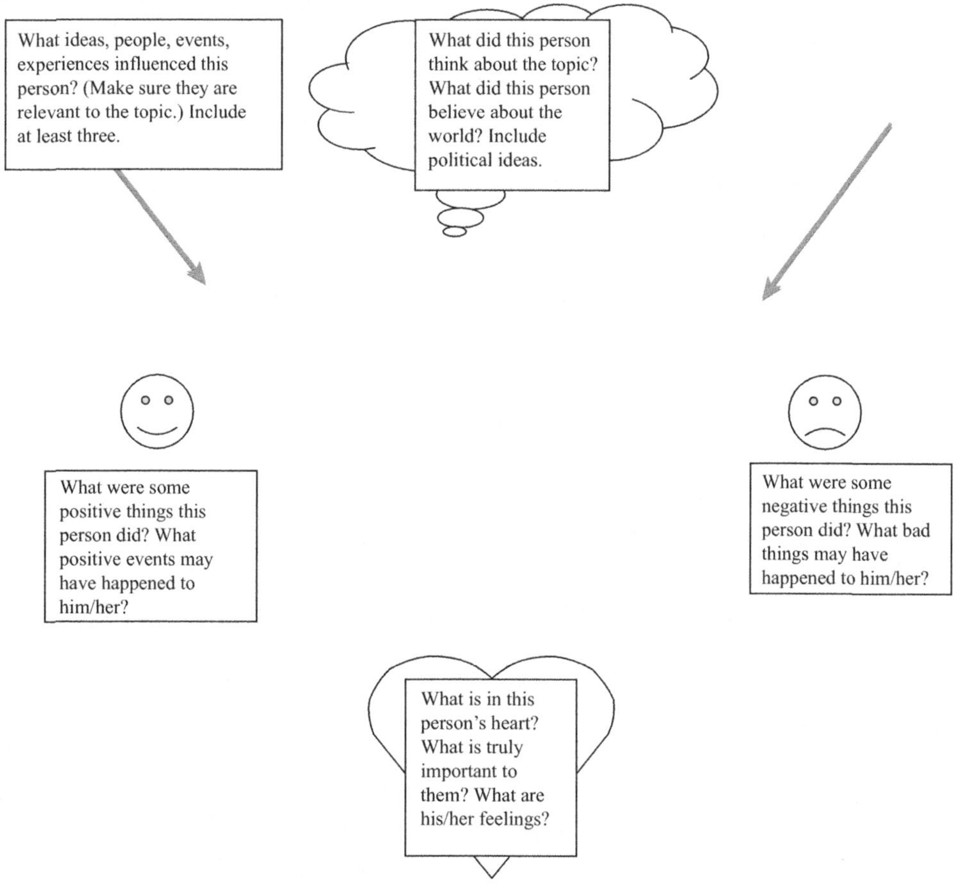

What ideas, people, events, experiences influenced this person? (Make sure they are relevant to the topic.) Include at least three.

What did this person think about the topic? What did this person believe about the world? Include political ideas.

What were some positive things this person did? What positive events may have happened to him/her?

What were some negative things this person did? What bad things may have happened to him/her?

What is in this person's heart? What is truly important to them? What are his/her feelings?

used it in U.S. History. Invariably, students who research Thomas Jefferson have a heck of a time if they run into any information on Sally Hemings (the slave whom Jefferson is thought to have fathered children with). They really have to decide for themselves if they plan on judging him through a twenty-first century perspective, or whether to allow for some leeway based on his historical context—but *they* have to do this evaluation, and sometimes they really, really take it to heart. Are they challenged while doing this body bio? For sure, both academically and analytically. They have to truly think, synthesize all they have read, and evaluate their findings in order to place them on the body bio itself. So are they engaged? Yes, this kind of active research engages them.

Additionally, they have the opportunity to use the research in myriad ways. For the body bios that students do for the Revolutionary War, they engage in a "Walk and Talk," where they interview each other on their motivations for being on the side they are on. For the body bios of the founders that they study (Hamilton, Adams, Madison, and Jefferson), they engage in a Facebook-esque conversation using Edmodo profiles and chats about such topics as the National Bank, the Alien and Sedition Acts, the Great Compromise, and political affiliations.

Whether your body bio assignment culminates in a Walk and Talk, a presentation, a project, a speech, a movie, a wax museum, or something else, just having students go through the process of compiling the information gives them a more complex, nuanced view of the historical figure than they would have just researching the usual details of a historical figure's life.

Presidents' Day

An example of when I use body biographies that result in research shared with a larger audience is Presidents' Day. We do an assembly that highlights students' research and shares information about the past presidents of the United States. Note that this kind of assembly opportunity presents itself at other times of the year, too. And while Presidents' Day is a natural companion to U.S. History class, an Ancient Civilizations or World History teacher could also create a day in which students share what they know with younger students or with an even larger audience through streaming or simulcasting.

The end result of the Presidents' Day preparations is a large room full of students dressed in suits and/or in their interpretation of what their president might have worn at that time. There is the usual cotton-ball wig for Washington, the interesting cravat for Franklin Pierce, the stovepipe hat for

Lincoln, and the wheelchair, borrowed from the nurse, for Franklin Delano Roosevelt. But despite these standard costumes, students make this day their own. The idea is that each president is re-running for office. They glad-hand the younger students and try to convince them why they are the best candidate to run.

In this activity, they have to carefully shape the research that they have done into more positive angles. For example, one year "Richard Nixon" stated in reference to the Watergate scandal that he "may have done some things wrong, but I've learned my lesson and would never do them again." Students need to look at both the positives and negatives of their figure's presidency and figure out why they should be president again. Then, there are the students who are concerned: They aren't sure their person *should* be president again. You'd think that these comments would be based on political views they've learned from their parents, but it's often presidents like Harding, Buchanan, Fillmore, or Taft ("But he doesn't even really *want* to be president!") who get this treatment. Students also struggle with William Henry Harrison, who infamously caught pneumonia on his inauguration day and succumbed about thirty days later—his presidency, then, was less than memorable.

In preparing for Presidents' Day, students face the usual research challenge of preparing the body biography and the evaluations that it entails. They struggle still with "Is this a good or bad thing?" and have to look closely at some of the most interesting events in the country's history. Then, from there, they craft a speech explaining why they should be president again. They bring a truncated version of their speech, along with fliers, buttons, posters, and any other campaign paraphernalia, to the assembly as they transform into the presidents of the United States for their younger peers.

The fact that this activity has an authentic audience, and that students use their research for a purpose, helps students later connect their learning to these presidents' actions as we study them in context in history class.

Field Trips

Field trips have historically been used to engage students. When I taught third grade, we were lucky enough to culminate our study of the Tongva Native American tribe by going to the Southwest Museum in Los Angeles and by going on a retreat where we built structures called wikiups and did other activities. These culminating activities can be awesome ways for students to really see what they have spent so much time learning about.

While there is some disagreement amongst educators as to whether field trips should occur before a unit of study or after it, most educators agree that field trips are great. However, they are in decline. Why? Jay P. Greene et al., in an article for *Education Next* (2013) about the value of field trips, argue that a lack of finances, time constraints, and an increased focus on standardized testing all make it less likely for teachers and administrators to fight for the field trip. This is despite the fact that, as Greene et al. observe in their article, students have a high level of recall from the events and facts they experience during a field trip.

So we know that, when possible, students should be going on field trips and the trips should be related to the content they are studying. These trips can be a way for students to experience what they have researched and explored in class, or a way for them to get a taste of what they *will* be studying in the classroom before they even start. I really like the idea of a field trip as kick-off to activate interest for a unit, but this can be a challenge if the field trip location's workers are not used to introducing students to a topic. Often docent volunteers are still rooted in the question-response fishing protocols and will be flummoxed and possibly offended if students don't come prepared to the museum trip. Of course, no matter when in a unit of study students visit a site, they *should be* prepared as to the deco-rum of speaking respectfully to docents, behaving themselves at the site itself, and following the rules of both the school and the field trip site. Also, if you decide to have students visit a site before teaching about it, be pre-pared to explain this to the museum ahead of time, or at least to the docents on the tour so that they understand that you aren't trying to be disrespect-ful of their time, but rather are trying to give your students a preview, a taste of what they will be studying—a visual or tactile experience that they can refer back to during the unit.

Depending on where you live, there may be an amazing fount of resources at your disposal. This also depends, too, on the content you are studying. Living and teaching in Los Angeles, I am lucky enough to have access to the Bowers Museum, which for a time held a portion of the Terra-cotta Army of Emperor Qin Shi Huang of China; the Los Angeles Natural History Museum, which houses various exhibits on the history of California; the Autry Museum, which focuses on the American West; the Skirball Cul-tural Center, which has an interesting archaeology experience for Ancient Civilizations students; the Reagan Library, which rotates various exhibits that can be useful for history teachers; and the Huntington, which recently had an exhibit on the Constitution. As a U.S. History teacher, though, sometimes I wish I could live and teach closer to Philadelphia, New York, Boston, Virginia, or Washington, D.C., or at least take trips there to show my students the history contained in those places.

Virtual Field Trips

So when you can't go to a place because of its location, there is another option, thanks to ever-improving technology. I'm talking about the virtual field trip. Not every museum or cultural site has this option, but they are increasing in number as I type this. It's especially important to give students virtual access to cultural sites if they can't visit locations on their own for socio-economic reasons or due to their location. The Smithsonian Museums have virtual field trip options, as does Ellis Island. So do the National Museum of Natural History, the Louvre, Mt. Vernon, Colonial Williamsburg, and the U.S. Capitol. There is a virtual tour available of China's Forbidden City, and of the historic center of Urbino to study the Renaissance (see Appendix A for a list of museums and cultural centers offering virtual field trips). It's worth searching to see what virtual tours might match up with one of your units of study.

While it is true that field trips can take time and money, it is worth it for students to be able to experience concepts and see things firsthand, or, at least virtual-hand. In fact, these virtual field trips can be incorporated into students' presentations, or can be taken as a whole class, or if the technology is available, can be taken at home to share the learning with families. These field trips, whether taken in a physical or virtual reality, can produce a sense of awe and wonder about the past—a sense of the oldness and *awe*someness of what from the past still exists today. Even middle schoolers, who are often so hard to impress, feel this awe.

> Field trips ... can produce a sense of awe and wonder about the past—a sense of the oldness and *awe*someness of what from the past still exists today. Even middle schoolers, who are often so hard to impress, feel this awe.

Games

Gamification is a big thing in education right now. There are proponents who say that gamifying the classroom is the answer to educational malaise—that it mirrors the striving and the immediate reward payoff that students are so motivated to engage with. Then, there are teachers who are wary of bringing video games, or learning experiences that mirror the idea of video games, into their own teaching. These teachers would say that students need to develop an internal system of intrinsic rewards, and that life does not mirror video games. Other teachers, while interested in games, might be wary of "throwing out" an entire curriculum in favor of a system based on principles of gamification. I, personally, am waiting to see where this all goes. While I am very happy to embrace the principles of project-based learning, I have less of a personal affinity to some of the tenets of game play. My brother, nine years younger than I, has been gaming since he could pick up a controller. I, on the other hand, wasn't allowed to have a Nintendo growing up, so gaming isn't really a language that I am familiar speaking.

However, I see some of the benefits—and the number one benefit is engagement. Students are often engaged and learn a great deal from educational games. I will give examples of games in the classroom, but they aren't part of a larger gamification program.

One of the games that I use from time to time is a Choose Your Own Adventure type game that my collaborator Shara Peters wrote while she was in her teaching internship year. I remember it took her forever to compile the options and collate them into a logical sequence with options for the players. The idea behind her game, part of a unit on Immigration in the Progressive Era (which I will refer back to again in this chapter), was that the protagonist was an immigrant and, as in history, the fates facing him were myriad. Students choose which job they think will be a good choice, only to be foiled by Tammany Hall later, or they choose a job at a factory and join a union. This type of game allows students to get into the experience of pretending to be someone in history and feeling like there are stakes to be able to succeed (although the stakes can't be compared to reality). Students remember these types of experiences, and they enjoy them: engagement and enjoyment unlocked!

Game Creation

As I made clear in the previous section, gaming, though I respect it, is not quite my thing. So some of the best times games that have been put to use in my classroom have been when the students created the games. I've never assigned students to all produce games on one particular concept or piece of content (thought that could be an interesting thing to try), but whenever I've asked students to choose how they want to demonstrate understanding of a topic, some students do pick game creation.

Students have created games on the Revolutionary War, games matching the geographical cutouts of slave/free/border states during the Civil War, games showing the causes of the Civil War (the conceit of this one was that every time something happened that catalyzed the war, players had to move their piece backwards), and a game called Civil War Weaponopoly that showed the different kinds of technological advancements in weaponry during the Civil War and how they affected the war itself.

Game creation requires students to represent large concepts with detail. They have to create rules, marry concepts and contents, and analyze human motivation. It's so much better that students create the games themselves and then have their peers play them. They have to work hard to synthesize the concepts they've learned, and apply, fail, reiterate, and then hopefully succeed in creating an interesting experience that both engages the creator and the player.

Simulations

Simulations are another type of engaging activity. They can be interesting, but we need to exercise great care when using them—mainly because there are certain historical events that we just cannot replicate or simulate, nor would we want to—and to suggest that we can would be often offensive to those who endured the historical events. Examples of these events to avoid are slavery, the Holocaust, the Japanese internment of World War II, the Armenian Genocide, the Rwandan Genocide . . . you get the picture.

I do have my students read excerpts from Solomon Northup's autobiography *Twelve Years a Slave* and then clean raw cotton as an ancillary experience to discussing the counterintuitive impact that the cotton gin had on slaves and the cotton economy of the south, but I make a point to tell students that by no means are we simulating slavery. To clean cotton is not to experience slavery in the slightest.

There are times we might want to discuss the drawbacks of simulations with students but then give them a try so students can use their imaginations to connect to people who lived through history.

These simulations are only limited by the students' and teacher's imaginations. For instance, students can simulate being members of Greek city states and, in those city states, have particular roles. I remember in my seventh grade class, I was the Oracle of Delphi and sat under a table. I remember this lesson, and I remember being excited about history and being engaged in history. Students can recreate trials, important government decisions, falls and rises of empires around the world, and ancient civilization interconnectivity.

Shara Peters, whom I mentioned earlier, made a simulation of the creation of a labor union in a garment factory. It was all things a simulation should be: messy, educational, and engaging. Students were given character cards and instructions as to how to do their work (to simulate garment cutting, they were asked to fold and cut paper in a particular way). Then one student, pre-chosen, got up and explained why she/he thought that they should organize and create a labor union, citing the historically infamous Triangle Shirtwaist Fire that was conveniently placed as a news item in their "newspaper." Students mentioned other instances, like no breaks and locking the doors during work hours. When students shared their opinions, based on their character cards, it got chaotic, but at least it was historically engaged chaos. They played their parts and they remembered why people spoke up and created labor unions.

Revolutionary War Simulation

Another simulation that Shara and I worked on together was the Revolutionary War simulation. This could work for any battle where the two sides had particularly different tools for battle, different tactics for fighting, different geographical advantages/disadvantages, etc.

For this battle, I would place two-thirds of the students on the British side (to better represent the troop advantages the British had), and the remaining students on the side of the patriots/colonists/rebels (depending on the perspective). Students would then be given particular rules: All soldiers on either side have to scrunch their piece of paper ten times in order to simulate the time it would take to load a musket. The students on the British side have to wait until their commander tells them that they can fire, and they must all stand in a line. The patriot side, however, gets to hide in the playground equipment and fire whenever they please. We talk about this being an oversimplification of the guerilla vs. organized fighting styles of each side, but it does get the point across.

Students then engage in the battle. Often, because they are middle schoolers, they cheat, and then they tell on others for cheating. Some complain that this one didn't scrunch the paper (ammo) ten times before firing, or that this one was hit by a paper and never "got out." Students tend to really let it out when they are debriefing the battle. The British side often hates firing in the lines (except in years when their commander is particularly commanding and strong), but they can see why, in some cases, it could be an advantage based on the problem of aiming the muskets. The Patriot side often feels unfairly handicapped, too, based on their smaller numbers. Ultimately, we talk about how this particular war was a war of attenuation—that America wore down British resources enough to be too much of a problem to bother with any longer (and the inclusion of the French didn't hurt either). But what students really get out of the battle is often more poignant than those facts.

Last year, a student said in the debrief that he could imagine, for a second, how scared soldiers might have been, standing in those lines and waiting for musket fire. Middle schoolers are still kids—they still have access to the imaginative play component of themselves that we as adults often lose. Simulations, like I said earlier, cannot come close to simulating actual historical events, but they can activate that part of a middle schooler's brain, the self that can imagine what things might have been like in the past, in a particular historical situation. They just need the opportunity to be able to pretend. Will they remember every historical detail based on just doing a simulation? Probably not, but the odds of them remembering *all* the important historical details are not that high no matter what vehicle is used for the conveyance. They can look up all the details anyway, if they need them. They will, however, remember a feeling, a fleeting connection to people from the past that may have felt similar emotions. These connections engage not only their minds but their imaginations as well.

> Middle schoolers are still kids—they still have access to the imaginative play component of themselves that we as adults often lose. Simulations . . . can activate that part of a middle schooler's brain . . .

Engaging the Unique Qualities of Middle Schoolers

The unique nature of middle school students can be a challenge or an asset, depending on the situation. They are not always going to engage in work simply because they are told to do so. Even the most diligent, hard-working middle schoolers may have times when their "classroom engagement" switch is cut off in favor of other kinds of engagement, like figuring out their social lives and exploring new feelings toward family, self, and friends.

Students need to work and be busy at school, no question. But they also need engaging activities and tasks that will help them shift away from preoccupation with self and into a historical mindset. It isn't always simple to do this, and just because an activity is fun for students, doesn't mean that it has lasting value. Conversely, just because something isn't fun, doesn't mean that it isn't important to learn.

Students need to learn skills. They also need to connect to history in deeper ways. That happens when we give them autonomy to evaluate and make decisions about history for themselves (as with the body bios), and when we help them experience the "past-ness" of history in a visual and tactile way through field trips, real or virtual, or by activating their imaginations through simulations.

Middle school students still like to play, and they like to imagine. They want to be treated with respect as human beings who are learning how to be more autonomous, but they are still sometimes scared of that autonomy. They are eager to be more grown up—for example, I find that sixth graders are not impressed by stickers because they want to prove that they aren't little kids any longer, but *eighth* graders love stickers because they know they are still kids/or they know they aren't anymore and want to recapture the feeling. You can have both in a class—kids who have legitimately crossed that line and have grown up, and kids who aren't quite there yet.

> Middle school students . . . want to be treated with respect as human beings who are learning how to be more autonomous, but they are still sometimes scared of that autonomy.

It's a hard age, but one where the contradictions can be harnessed and used for academic and social emotional good. When middle schoolers can feel empathy toward historical figures through simulation or research, they are practicing for real life. They are also engaged in the study of history—not just intellectually, but emotionally too. Students of this age can still close their eyes and imagine being in the past, imagine being someone else—somewhere else—in the world. It is this sense of imagination, readily available in elementary school students, that is fleetingly caught and harnessed in the middle school student. However, this imagination, combined with the new skills and abilities, makes middle schoolers *amazing* candidates for engagement in the history classroom. They can do more than elementary school students intellectually, while still holding onto the childish imagination that high schoolers have often grown out of. So it's our job to capture it—to allow middle school students the autonomy they deserve and crave, while still allowing for play and for deep emotional engagement in the classroom.

Chapter 7 Self-Reflection

1. What field trips do you take in history class? Which would you take if time and resources weren't part of the equation?
2. How do you see the unique nature of middle school students reflected in your classroom?
3. What strategies do you use to engage students in thinking about the past?
4. What strategies from this chapter are you thinking of utilizing?
5. What adjustments might you need to make for your own classroom and the needs of your students?

References

Greene, Jay P., Brian Kisida, and Daniel H. Bowen. "The Educational Value of Field Trips." *Education Next RSS*. Education Next, 15 Sept. 2013. Web. 7 Sept. 2015.

Vygotsky, L. S. *Mind in Society: The Development of Higher Psychological Processes*. Cambridge: Harvard University Press, 1978. Print.

8

Inquiry

Project-Based Learning

Summative Projects or Project-Based Learning?

Imagine this: Students walk into the classroom, wave hello to the teacher, and look around for their team members. Then they immediately get out what they need and begin working with their team. They are independent, motivated, confident, and *learning*.

This is not the permanent state of my classroom. This is my vision. But I have seen it happen at times, and those moments were only achieved when my students were in the midst of a project-based learning inquiry.

In my years in the classroom, I've done both summative projects and project-based learning. While both of these project styles can allow students to integrate disciplines and express their understanding through alternate means, there are definite differences between the two approaches.

Summative projects enable students to showcase what they've learned during a unit by creating a project. The project may or may not include elements of choice; the level of choice is primarily dictated by the teacher. Conversely, **project-based learning** (PBL) usually has fewer parameters, is primarily driven by students' investigation and inquiry, and often revolves around a large question that students are charged to explore. Larmer, Mergendoller, and

Boss explain that project-based learning is a process in which students use inquiry methods to investigate a complex issue or problem and gain skills and content as part of that process (2015). Often, as recommended by Ron Berger, author of *An Ethic of Excellence* (2003), there is an authentic audience for the project.

Advocates of project-based learning may espouse particular formats. Long-time PBL practitioners who have been crafting projects for their students for years will have strong opinions about how to go through each step of creating and executing a project. But the truth is that for any teacher trying PBL, there will some trial and error and some customization that will likely be necessary to make it work well for the teacher and students.

With middle school students, project-based learning can be a lifesaver, but it can also be a unique challenge. As discussed earlier, middle schoolers need rigor and work outside their Zone of Proximal Development (Vygotsky, 1978), but they need support as well. They want to be in charge of their own learning, but they often need assistance. They aren't always equipped developmentally or experientially with a foundation of historical knowledge upon which to learn new concepts, events, or ideas, and they often need teachers to help them contextualize new information. Therefore, these projects can be prime opportunities for us to provide supported autonomy, in-depth inquiries with scaffolded context, and academically challenging tasks that allow students to showcase what they know through means other than standardized tests or written responses.

> Projects can be prime opportunities for us to provide supported autonomy, in-depth inquiries with scaffolded context, and academically challenging tasks that allow students to showcase what they know through means other than standardized tests or written responses.

To that end, this chapter examines three projects I've done in my eighth-grade classroom that utilize elements of project-based learning—each with different modes and objectives. Each of these projects can be adapted for any grade-level content, and each requires students to reach, learn new skills, and activate some of the "middle school-ness" of themselves—in other words, to put part of themselves in the project so that they can more readily make connections with the content and with the larger world. They'll share their findings with others, too, and will gain some academic skills along the way.

Project #1: Welcome to Class, Now Build Yourself a Country: Government Types Project

Government Types Project

Your assignment:

Create a country/community that is governed by the type of government you are given.

You must describe:

How rules are created.
How rules are enforced.
The role of the government.
The role of the people.
The size of your country.

You must

◆ Write a description that includes a definition.
◆ Create something that shows who has the power in your government.

One of the most challenging aspects of project-based learning in middle school is its open-endedness. While such projects could be scary at any age, they're especially intimidating to pre-teens/early teens. There's something about that age that makes an open-ended project a vast, frightening experience—a place where one can be judged harshly for unique choices. Each time students are asked to make open-ended decisions, they're weighing the perceived value judgments of their peers.

I find that at the beginning of the year, my main goal of a project is really just to help students get over this self-doubt and this worry about what others are thinking. That goal even takes precedence over the content itself.

Origins: Just Trying to Teach about Government Types Here

This lesson falls at the beginning of the year—a kick-off to the Constitution unit. This particular lesson has had a long history in my curriculum; I developed it after I realized that in order for students to understand arguments that occurred during the creation of the Constitution (about the balances of power between the federal and state governments and the individual), they would need to understand how different governments worked. In the lesson's first iteration, I gave students a line to use as a spectrum (on one side, government has the power, and on the other, people have the power) and had students place images and text that represented different government types on that spectrum. This was done as a whole class and was often a bit of a free-for-all. I knew that I wanted to make this lesson more student-centered, and so I decided to make it more project-based.

The Process

Since I do this lesson at the beginning of the year, it would be too much for students to face an entirely open-ended project. I assign each team of students a particular government type (communism, democracy, republic, anarchy, dictatorship, monarchy, oligarchy), rather than give them a choice. However, they do have choice in terms of what they *do* with the government type. When I assign this project, I often introduce it with this preface:

> "Some of you will really love that you can do anything with this project, and for some of you it will really freak you out. If you are someone who usually likes to have the teacher tell you exactly what to do, this might freak you out at first. But, I have never had a student not be able to do it. You've just got to sit with the uncomfortable feeling of not knowing what you are going to do. That's when you will get an awesome idea. And then you will know."

It's a long speech, but it's necessary for emotional scaffolding. Middle schoolers often want to fit in. When they feel a certain emotion, they worry that they are the *only ones in the whole world* who have ever had that feeling, and that everyone else in the room is cool and totally comfortable. I make sure to tell them that they aren't the only ones and, moreover, that they will get through it. Additionally, I point out that their feeling of being uncomfortable is often an important part of the process of creating something. I want students to gain from these projects the experience of having gone through that uncomfortable part of

> I want students to gain from these projects the experience of having gone through that uncomfortable part of the design process. To create is not always comfortable, but the process is almost always worthwhile.

the design process. To create is not always comfortable, but the process is almost always worthwhile.

Working in Teams

In teams, students research their government type and then go about creating a country that utilizes that government type. Listening to the conversations between students can be informative—or it can be painful. Many students at this age need help, either with stepping up to advocate for their own ideas, or with stepping back to give others a chance to share.

Before this project begins, I have students reflect on "who they are" as group workers, what they like about group work, and what they think they might need to work on. After this, we discuss group effectiveness as a class. This metacognitive activity helps students focus more on their own role in the team dynamic, but it is certainly not a silver bullet. It is always a challenge for us as middle school teachers to give kids the space to work out their ideas together, while making sure that they are being respectful of one another. If a group is struggling, we will talk out the process together— the process of the struggle (and hopefully overcoming it) is a learning experience—but it is difficult for students to have that kind of foresight in the moment.

The Challenge of Choice

So what are these teams arguing about? Often it is *how* to convey what they know—what medium they are going to choose to present their country. Some students may really want to make a movie; others might also want to make a movie but have it be stop-motion. Regardless, the conflict needs to be reconciled and the project's medium agreed upon. When there is so much choice available, students can feel overwhelmed (and I rarely like to give them examples—I know some teachers swear by examples, but I can't shake the feeling that they take away from what could be). When students get overwhelmed, I go back to my earlier speech. I remind them that being unsure and being uncomfortable are part of the design process. Sometimes what they wanted to do doesn't work, and they have to go back to the drawing board; this also can cause conflict within teams. However, this challenge of choice is often ameliorated by the fact that students *are* in teams. I find that their brainstorming process seems to be much more fruitful, and the sullen "I don't know what to do" portion of the activity seems to be much shorter when there is collaboration involved, rather than students being confronted by so much choice while working individually.

The Results

The results for a project like this are twofold. First are the tangible results. For example, one team made a movie in which they introduced their community and all the people who worked in it, including descriptions of what their jobs were and who held the power within the community. Another team created a monument to their dictator with Legos, developing a backstory about the dictator's rules and regulations for the country. The other type of result is more intangible: the awareness that they can handle choice and can trust themselves. When I first assign this, there is often a flurry of students asking, "Is it OK if we do ____?" My answer is always, "Does it show your government type? If so, yes." But after a while, they start to internalize this answer. Subsequently, they start trusting that I trust *them* to demonstrate their learning and demonstrate their learning with quality. They realize through this project that although they have choice, they have to make *thoughtful* decisions because I have high expectations for them as both team players and as individuals. And they start to trust themselves a bit more, too.

Looking beyond the Content: What Is the Value for Middle School Students?

When my students went back to place the distinct government types on the spectrum after engaging in the project, they seemed to have a much firmer grasp of the balance of power between the government and the people than they did when I had taught the lesson previously without the project component. Why? Because it was theirs now. The tinkering, ideating, designing, and choosing that went on for each team allowed students to connect the learning to their own interests and experiences. In my experience, if middle schoolers are able to learn something of political and historical import on their own terms, they are much more likely to internalize its meaning. Using Erikson's model of the psychosocial stages of development (1959), students in middle school are moving from the tension between industry vs. inferiority to identity vs. role confusion. The student may still be mastering this idea of industry or inferiority, or it may still be the tension that is motivating him or her—which is why many struggle with the open-endedness of certain projects. Identity issues are also added into the mix. Students are

Students are just beginning to differentiate themselves and their ideas from that of their parents and teachers, so giving them choices can help them see that being allowed to make decisions on their own isn't a *problem*, but a chance for them to explore who they are and who they want to be.

just beginning to differentiate themselves and their ideas from that of their parents and teachers, so giving them choices can help them see that being allowed to make decisions on their own isn't a *problem*, but a chance for them to explore who they are and who they want to be.

Having to tackle the collaborative aspect of a project is also an asset for students rather than simply a challenge—although it *is* a challenge, because students are developing their limbic systems, i.e. the part of the brain that seeks to make relationships (Giedd, 2015). We might as well give students opportunities to work within these relationships and gain from others, rather than sequester each student at his or her desk. You have to know your audience, and an audience of middle schoolers often needs to be drawn into content through this focus on relationships and choice.

Project #2: Parameters and Scaffolding: Civil War Technology Project

Civil War Technology

Your assignment:

- ◆ In teams, create a project that examines an answer(s) to this question: How did your technology change the Civil War?
- ◆ Your project must fully answer the question and be beautiful, meaningful, sophisticated, and enduring (adapted from Gary Stager, n.d.).

Once my students have had a taste of how autonomy, choice, and projects work in the class, it is much easier to move from a project-based learning lesson that spans three days to one that encompasses the learning of an entire unit's curriculum.

Origins: Project-Based Learning as an Opportunity for Independence

I've noticed my middle school students often struggle, not necessarily with meeting expectations, but with meeting expectations *independently*—without assistance and without validation for tasks they are able to do. Now, I believe that most have the tools to meet expectations independently—and I am not talking about taking out scaffolding in favor of throwing students into the deep-end—but the problem is that often, my students ask for reassurance and assistance regardless of whether they *actually* need it or not.

Project-based learning in this regard can be a great antidote to student doubt and a lack of self-efficacy. It would be a challenge to fail something where there isn't one correct way to do it. For the students who needs constant check-ins, validation, and reassurance from the teacher, project-based learning *is* a challenge, but a liberating one that will require them to step out of their comfort zones and develop trust in themselves to master content and create something unique.

> For the students who needs constant check-ins, validation, and reassurance from the teacher, project-based learning *is* a challenge, but a liberating one that will require them to step out of their comfort zones and develop trust in themselves to master content and create something unique.

Challenge: Parameters, Yea or Nay?

For a number of years now, my students have been engaging with the concept of the Civil War through the idea of Civil War technology. They've been working through the inquiry question: "How did the technology change the war?" While undistilled project-based learning often removes parameters from the inquiry process, I have found that with middle schoolers, some parameters are necessary, or at least helpful. It's hard to find the right ratio of how much support to how much autonomy students will need/have for any given project. In an attempt to address students' need for increased autonomy, while still scaffolding emotional and academic learning so that they can be successful, I've done some trial and error to create a bit of a hybrid PBL project.

Solution: Timing and Skills

By design, this inquiry/PBL unit occurs toward the end of the school year. By this point, the academic scaffolding—how to effectively research, how to analyze whether a site is credible or not (using Common Sense Media's Test before You Trust checklist https://www.commonsensemedia.org/educa tors/lesson/identifying-high-quality-sites-6-8), how to cite sources, how to paraphrase, how to search for primary and secondary sources, and how to create an open ended project—has already been put in place. This is imperative, because often the more open-ended an inquiry is and the more open-ended the results expected from the students, the more insecure they can become about their abilities, especially at this age. If students have had previous successes with many or most of the components required for the project, then they will feel a greater sense of self-efficacy and assuredness that they can follow the project to fruition, regardless of setbacks and re-iterations in the inquiry and design process.

Solution: Check-Ins

After a few years without it, I now provide students with a tool to help them be both autonomous *and* supported in their inquiry quest. It is a checklist that I tell them is a guide for their process (see Table 8.1).

They can use it or not, but as I often remind them, if there is a point on the checklist that they haven't addressed in their project, it is likely that they *ought* to. For example, the checklist prompts students to search for primary and secondary sources, glean relevant information from those sources, paraphrase and compile the information, create a works cited page, discuss their answer to the inquiry question, choose a project format that works with their answer, and finally create a project. These steps help them see what the end-game is, when their only given rubric is to create a project that fully answers the question and that is beautiful, meaningful, sophisticated, and enduring. In previous units, without this checklist, some of the important skills that one would imagine a student would need to utilize weren't always used, and the projects suffered as a result.

Solution: Context

Content-wise, this unit is book-ended by units on Causes of the Civil War and Reconstruction. Students, before going into this unit, will have historical context for the conflict and the events that preceded it; they are ready to look at the way this war was different, both in terms of the technological advances and how some of these technological changes symbolize the conflict itself.

Table 8.1 Checklist for Civil War Technology Project

Assignment	Helpful Sites	Point Person	What Still Needs to be done	Other Notes	Date Completed
Find Primary Sources (writings, pictures from that time period) about your topic.	Library of Congress http://www.loc.gov/topics/content.php?subcat=8 SweetSearch http://www.sweetsearch.com				
Find Secondary Sources (writings and pictures others wrote about things from that time period) about your topic.	SweetSearch http://www.sweetsearch.com				
Create a works cited page	Easybib http://www.easybib.com See also citation page on Haiku				
Read then pull out & organize important information from primary and secondary sources					
Choose method of project: iMovie, presentation, model, other	Aurasma https://www.aurasma.com PechaKucha style Powerpoint https://en.wikipedia.org/wiki/PechaKucha				
Create project					
Craft presentation: Make sure that your presentation is: Interesting Engaging Concise					

The Process

To start the project, students first are introduced through video about the different types of Civil War technology innovations. From there, they select their level of interest in communication, medicine, espionage, weaponry, maritime warfare, and food innovation, and are placed in teams accordingly. This choice of topic allows them to have further buy-in, since they are able to choose something that interests them. Then, after I give an overview of the project and expectations, a reminder about citing sources, and a link to the checklist, students are ready to answer the question: "How did (their group's type of technology) change the Civil War?" The ultimate curricular goal is for students to be able to see, through their own inquiry, that the Civil War's devastation was, in part, due to fighting the current war in the same strategic terms as the last war; the increased innovations in technology made it more and more deadly to fight in the same ways. However, the intangible goals are as important as the content goals.

Each year, there is a wide variety of project types: some students blog, some write plays, some create presentations, some make Civil War food, some create movies, and many use technologies and applications such as TinkerCad to create models of Civil War warships or weapons.

Each year, though, a group doing Civil War communication invariably attempts to make their own telegraph. This is always one of the most interesting processes to watch. For middle schoolers, combining the tactile with the intellectual, mixed with the social exercise of working in teams, really creates a learning environment in which their understandings go beyond content.

These teams are able to see firsthand not only how the telegraph changed the war by communicating messages faster and farther than previously possible, but also how the process of creating something often has multiple iterations, trials, and errors, and is not necessarily a linear process.

The Results: It's as Much about the Process as It Is about the Knowledge

Each year, the Civil War communication team must iterate in order to be able to create an actual working telegraph. Frequently, I've noticed that the communication team starts by planning to make a *model* of a telegraph; however, after working for some time, they often decide that they are going to attempt to make a machine that *actually* works.

These iterations are one of the valuable components of PBL in the social studies classroom. One year, the students' first iteration didn't work because they didn't have anything magnetic, so they went back to the drawing board.

They needed to figure out how their insulated wires would work, and how metal needs to touch metal. In an effort to find something that would be magnetic, they took the metal part of my safety scissors to build the conductor. With effort and problem solving, and with trial and error, they made a functioning telegraph.

Looking beyond the Content: What Is the Value for Middle School Students?

During these middle years, students can learn a great deal, not just about a historical concept, but also about perseverance and their own ability to fail and succeed, to change plans, and to follow a project to its end. These are life skills that will help them (one hopes) in high school and beyond. Projects are often more valuable than the content or inquiry they address or represent; they often stand in for a real process of integration between disciplines, of creation, and of real work. Project-based learning isn't a one-size-fits-all pedagogy, or just an educational buzzword. It can be a way for students to differentiate a task to their own abilities, to gain experience in autonomous thought, and to stretch themselves. It's also a way for us as teachers to assess for understanding in a non-traditional way. For students, it is an *experience* of the growth mindset that Carol Dweck speaks about in her book *Mindset: The New Psychology of Success* (2006). Project-based learning can be an opportunity for students to embrace challenges, and to gain an understanding that their hard work and feelings of self-efficacy are goals in and of themselves.

> Project-based learning isn't a one-size-fits-all pedagogy, or just an educational buzzword. It can be a way for students to differentiate a task to their own abilities, to gain experience in autonomous thought, and to stretch themselves. It's also a way for us as teachers to assess for understanding in a non-traditional way.

What Does the Research Say?

One of the most important components of the project is one that I only added into later iterations—scaffolding (such as the checklist mentioned earlier). This addition seems to be borne out by the research: "The master-apprentice relationship is used as an analogy for the teaching-learning situation . . . like masters, teachers should scaffold instruction by breaking down tasks; use modeling, prompting, and coaching to teach strategies for thinking and problem solving; and gradually release responsibility to the learner" (Blumenfeld et al., 1991). As the research shows, students may need some additional supports in order to make the most out of project-based learning. Additionally, as Grant and Branch note in their 2005 study of project-based learning in middle school: "sustained project-based learning is a not a simple task for teachers or students. . . . It is essential for teachers to comprehend how students will perform in these learning environments and recognize that students may be ill prepared." This would seem to indicate that any student who might be ill-prepared because of lack of previous experience with autonomous learning models would need scaffolding and perhaps more practice collaborating, combined with a gradual increase in autonomy in classroom tasks. The research supports the idea that project-based learning can be beneficial, but middle school students may need training wheels.

Project #3: Are We in the Deep End Yet?: Causes of the Civil War Unit

> ### What Caused the Civil War?
>
> **Your assignment:**
>
> ◆ In teams, research what caused the Civil War.
> ◆ Create something that shows/demonstrates what you found.

While the above project also deals with the Civil War, the similarities end there. With the Civil War technology project, I focused on the idea of providing parameters and scaffolding to help students through the inquiry process. This year, I introduced a new unit—completely project based, and with minimal scaffolding—centered on the question: What caused the Civil War?

The Origins

Previous iterations of this unit had been quite structured, guided, and not as student-centered. The causes for the Civil War were *given* and gone over systematically in class, specifically: slavery, the Missouri Compromise, the Compromise of 1850, the Fugitive Slave Act, the Kansas-Nebraska Act/Bleeding

Kansas, the Dred Scott Decision, and the Election of 1860. When I thought about whether to turn this unit into a project-based learning assignment, I had some concerns. For example, I wondered, *What if they didn't learn about each of these very important causes in their own research?* What I eventually realized is that if I were to deliver the Civil War causes by standard methods—lecture, followed by testing—it would be extremely unlikely that the students would remember each and every one of these causes by name two, five, or ten years later. If they found the causes out themselves and made their own case for one or more of these causes, then *that* might be something committed to long-term memory.

The Process: Change in motivation, retention

Like the government types project and Civil War tech unit, this project was also done in teams, but it required even more research. I have a timeline posted in the room with causes (the ones mentioned above), so students had a place to start. For a couple days, however, many students seemed a bit unmoored. Then, a few students started crowdsourcing a giant map of the United States on the IdeaPaint wall; this changed the classroom both physically and emotionally. Suddenly students were adding dates, places, and events up on the map, and students were connecting the things they learned in the previous unit about the expansion of the United States with what was happening politically and ideologically with the factions of the American people at that time. Students began to see for themselves the symbolic importance of the Missouri Compromise, and the role that the Mexican American War might have played in bringing in new territory to fight over. Students learned about Dred Scott, John Brown, and Lincoln. Though I had to cede control of the exact content and didn't "cover" each cause I believe is important, the students owned their own research, and the causes they uncovered, they discovered themselves. They reached out to historians on Twitter to get their perspectives as well, going beyond the walls of the classroom in the process. Their varied projects (including a video game, dominoes with causes written on each, movies, models, and interactive games) showed they understood that a number of causes were at the root of the event, and that most of those causes revolved around different stances on slavery as an institution.

The Results

What is our net gain from assigning an inquiry-focused project versus presenting the information in a more standard unit or lesson-plan format?

While it is true that we need to relinquish some control of the content in order to develop an inquiry project, it is worth it because our goal shouldn't be based on exhaustive memorization anyway. As an example, let me offer a story from my personal history. I remember learning about the Shakers in my own eighth-grade history class—a class that relied on the "lecture, reading, answering the questions in the back of the book, and then the take a weekly test" model—but that is basically *all* that I remember from that class. So it cannot be just content that motivates us. But although the content itself doesn't automatically lead students to make connections, when students do the *exploration* themselves, they become much more affected, involved, and engaged in that content. Content is not the goal, but an inquiry-focused project that connects content with the present has a very good chance of making lasting connections in students' minds.

Looking beyond the Content: What Is the Value for Middle School Students?

The skills that students learn in an inquiry project—i.e. one where there isn't as much guidance or scaffolding—may not be as academic in nature as the ones learned during an essay assignment. Regardless, students working with this type of project will learn how to work collaboratively in teams and how to negotiate the Internet and find what they need from credible sources. Students also learn how to plan, to iterate, and ultimately how to trust themselves. This is the self-efficacy component first discussed in the Civil War technology project. Another important component of an inquiry project is its ability to motivate. Being allowed to use technology, multimedia, and the digital tools in the classroom in a purposeful way for learning can help students be driven to discover more about the topic (Spires et al., 2012). Increased motivation and self-efficacy might be the main reason why projects for this age group are so compelling.

Why Projects in Middle School?

As was discussed in each of the three PBL examples, middle school students are unique. They are on the cusp of independence, but many of them are still in need of emotional and academic scaffolding in order to feel successful in the classroom. Much of middle school students' time is taken up with their growing emotional life. They are becoming conscious of themselves, and of their place and their activities within groups; as a result, academics are often shunted to the side. So to get the students to engage in the classroom, we need to find a good balance of rigor (so they feel like what they are doing isn't "babyish," and so the work is challenging enough that they feel like their brains are working hard), collaboration (so they are able to learn more about how to effectively navigate all these new relationships with a specific goal in mind), independence (so they feel like they are moving from the elementary grades to a place with more autonomy where they can trust the teacher), and scaffolding (so they know that you are there if they falter). Project-based learning can be a perfect way for middle school students to work on all of those things that are so important to making their learning relevant. They might just start to love history, because they get it *and* they can show it.

Inquiry through Project-Based Learning: Applying in Context

While many of the examples provided deal specifically with eighth grade content, the content can be shaped according to your own grade level. For example, the open-ended inquiry unit: "What caused the Civil War?" could be adapted to sixth or seventh grade curricula with a purposeful inquiry question about content, e.g. "What caused the decline of the Roman Empire?" "What was the relationship between the environment and ancient civilizations?" Teaching students skills like independence, collaboration, self-efficacy, and creativity should drive the project as much as the choice of content.

Depending on your teaching circumstances, you may be completely willing and able to take the plunge and turn one of your history units into a PBL inquiry unit, or perhaps you'll just want to change one or two lessons. The amount of technology at your disposal may play a role in how much project-based learning you're able to implement—while technology isn't a requirement, it is certainly a helpful tool in crafting and executing project-based learning units. Also, students may need additional scaffolding in literacy skills in order to work independently on parts of these projects. Additionally, the administration or district in your school may or may not be on board with such sweeping changes. These are all important things to consider, but the benefits we've discussed can be well worth the steps that need to be taken to implement them. If you're just getting started, remember that you can scaffold for yourself, not just for students! Take on the projects in small increments so you can learn along the way.

Chapter 8 Self-Reflection

1. What are your feelings about teacher vs. student centered classrooms?
2. Have you tried PBL in your classroom? How did it go?
3. What projects/project-based learning experiences do your students engage in during the year?
4. What strategies from this chapter are you thinking of utilizing?
5. What adjustments might you need to make for your own classroom and the needs of your students?

References

Berger, Ron. *An Ethic of Excellence: Building a Culture of Craftsmanship with Students*. Portsmouth, NH: Heinemann, 2003. Print.

Blumenfeld, P., Soloway, E., Marx, R., Krajcik, J., Guzdial, M., and Palincsar, A. *Motivating Project-Based Learning: Sustaining the Doing, Supporting the Learning*. Educational Psychologist 26 (1991): 369–398. Web. 27 July 2015.

Dweck, Carol S. *Mindset: The New Psychology of Success*. New York: Random House, 2006. Print.

"Erikson's Stages of Development." Learning Theories. N.p., 23 July 2014. Web. 27 July 2015.

Giedd, Jay N. "Risky Teen Behavior Is Driven by an Imbalance in Brain Development." *Scientific American Global RSS*. N.p., June 2015. Web. 27 July 2015.

Grant, Michael M., and Robert Maribe Branch. "Project-Based Learning in A Middle School: Tracing Abilities through the Artifacts of Learning." *Journal of Research on Technology in Education* 38.1 (2005): 65–98. ERIC. Web. 15 July 2015.

Larmer, John, John R. Mergendoller, and Suzie Boss. *Setting the Standard for Project Based Learning: A Proven Approach to Rigorous Classroom Instruction*. Virginia: ASCD, 2015. Print.

Spires, Hiller, Lisa G. Hervey, Gwynn Morris and Catherine Stelpflug. "Energizing Project-Based Inquiry: Middle-Grade Students Read, Write, and Create Videos." *Journal of Adolescent and Adult Literacy* 55.6 (2012): 483–493. Web. 15 July 2015.

Stager, Gary. "Raise Our Standards." *Creative Educator*, N.d. Web. 15 Dec. 2015. <http://www.thecreativeeducator.com/v06/articles/Raising_Our_Standards>.

Vygotsky, L. S. *Mind in Society: The Development of Higher Psychological Processes.* Cambridge: Harvard University Press, 1978. Print.

9

Assessment

The Changing Nature of Assessment

How can we tell if all of this we are doing is working? How can we tell if students are learning?

I recently had a ninth grade student come back and tell me that she feels "100 percent prepared for [her ninth grade] history class" because of history class last year. But this kind of report the white whale of feedback, is not usually forthcoming. So how can teachers assess what students are really retaining, and whether they are prepared for the next step in their education? Or whether they are prepared to apply the skills in class in their lives?

Assessment is possibly the most debated topic in education now. And the debate isn't limited to schools or individual educators or administrators; the government is involved—national, state, and local governments alike. In recent years, schools across the country have experienced the effects of increased higher-stakes standardized testing and have made accommodations within curricula to compensate (Walker, 2010). But standardized testing isn't the only change in assessment practice recently. There has also been more of a focus on assessing purposefully using both formative and summative assessments in order to better figure out what students are understanding and what content and skills they've retained from class.

Often, our expectations of students are wrapped up in curriculum that we create. We create and craft learning experience for students, and we expect certain things from them: we expect that classroom management will go well, we hope that students will engage with all the activities we create, and we hope they will participate in each and every learning experience that they themselves create and/or we provide. However, these expectations aren't always aligned with the realities of the classroom. Students are complex individuals—they are complicated academically, emotionally, and socially, and are affected by influences beyond their control: their families, living situations, socioeconomic level, safety, etc. Students are juggling multiple languages, or cultural environments, and are learning in the classroom not only content and skills, but also how to code-switch or learn another language for social as well as academic purposes. All of these things make it more rewarding, necessary, and important to teach, but they also complicate our ability as teachers to be able to assess one student the same way as the next.

Assessment in Middle School

Depending on the work norms of a particular middle school class, doing well can be seen as all important to the kids—a competition for who can do the best work—or, conversely, doing well can be seen as only for suckers, and wanting to do well marks you as a nerd or dork, or as whatever derogatory term the kids are calling each other these days. And it can easily go either way depending on the mix of kids in the class and the tone of the grade or the school as a whole. Most likely, each class will have a mix of kids on this particular spectrum: goody-goody to the too-cool-for-school.

So what's the problem with this? Middle school students cannot function individually within a vacuum. Assessment can bring out the group dynamics of a middle school: They compare what each of them got on a particular test, whether they tried too hard, whether they understood something, or whether they were "too dense" to get a concept. Before asking a question during a lesson, watch the room of middle schoolers. Each looks around, seemingly thinking: Is it OK if I answer this? How will my peers perceive me? Will I look dumb? Will they laugh at me and just say that they're only kidding even though they aren't? These are real questions that many middle schoolers ask themselves before making any academic decisions. Really, it's a wonder we get them to do anything in class.

If we want class to be a place where we can actually measure what students know, without there being too much influence from peer groups over students' academic decisions, then we need to set a tone for the class-room that makes students feel like they can take risks, even in assessment settings. They need to realize that if they can back up an assertion, then it's valid; there isn't always one right answer the teacher is looking for. They also have to feel that working hard and asking for help are group norms, not things to be embarrassed of—and that going over their work over and over isn't a waste of their time. These things are difficult to establish but are important if you want students to invest in the class and demonstrate the results of that investment.

> We need to set a tone for the class-room that makes students feel like they can take risks, even in assess-ment settings.

Making It Safe: Creating a Culture of Success

Our expectations as teachers, the ones that drive us to create a challenging and rigorous curriculum, are what students need to hear in order to want to succeed. There is debate about the value of internal vs. external moti-vation, but I've found that high teacher expectations (within the student's ZPD) can be a catalyst in increasing students' own internal motivation. If students believe that you truly believe they can succeed, they start believing it on their own. And if they *can* (and that "if" is often dependent on their academic and extenuating circumstances), their work will start reflecting those expec-tations. Will it work for all students? No. But you will get enough kids to feel like working hard is the group norm of the class. They will work for you, and they will work for themselves—an invaluable skill.

> If students believe that you truly believe they can succeed, they start believing it on their own.

But then, how do we ward off the overly competitive atmosphere that can come from students wanting to do well and receive external validation? It's tough. I spoke earlier in the book about my transparent gradebook, and even that can result in over-competitiveness in students—the grades are there and are so easy to share. When I first hear students start to compare grades, I tell them a story from college. I tell them about the time I was in an undergrad class, and every single time we got a paper back, the guy who sat behind me would ask "whadja get?" One day I had an epiphany. I realized that NO MATTER WHAT I responded, it wasn't good for either of us. Namely: if he did better than I did, *I* felt bad; if I did better than he did, he felt bad; plus, there's that slightly insidious feeling of *schadenfreude* (a term I explain to the students) when he's done worse than I have. Not only can I feel good about myself, but kind of good because *he* didn't do well. Or if I've done poorly, he gets to feel both good about himself and all that *schadenfreude*, too. That's not a great way to be in the world, if we can help it. The only *moderately* neutral result of this endgame would be if it were a draw somehow, and we both got the exact same grade. And then, what about next time?

Does this story change my students' lives? No way. I am not naive enough to think that every time I get on my soapbox, my students hang on to every word, but . . . they do mention schadenfreude when other kids ask, "What did you get?" So, it at least gives some students pause.

When I've assessed students in the past, especially in writing, I've noticed that I write a ton all over their papers and then nothing happens. Do they even read the corrections? This one-way communication was keeping students from feeling like agents of their own learning. I've started using Google Drive/Docs more and more for collaborative purposes. For any given writing assessments, students will turn in multiple drafts that we will discuss through Google Drive, so it's not just a one way, me commenting situation, but rather a dialogue—or, a chat, to use the parlance of our times. This kind of iterative process in writing, like in project creation, makes students feel like they have the skills to improve. This way, when they do have to do a standardized/timed writing assignment, they have the experiences of draft and revision and improvement to fall back on; they aren't making the same mistakes that they used to (one can hope). And, most importantly, they feel confident in their own skills.

Skills Scope and Sequence

So much of history class is content based. After all, it is *history*—it's the study of the past, the study of stuff, the study of peoples, cultures, civilizations, governments . . . Without all that, what is it? But the content, while of course important to measure, is only a component of what students need to know to be successful in history class.

Skills, specifically historical skills, are paramount in the Common Core State Standards. But it is difficult to assess for skills unless you've clearly articulated *what* skills you want students to be able to master by the end of middle school. To that end, Shara Peters and I created a scope and sequence, which we previously shared on MiddleWeb (http://www.middleweb.com/tag/history-scope-and-sequence/). It delineates the skills that we would hope our students would be able to master by each grade level. The scope and sequence assumes the presence of technology, which is not in all classrooms. However, these skills can be adjusted according to the makeup of the students and the tools at the teacher's disposal.

With this scope and sequence, students in sixth grade, who have come from elementary school and are at a developmentally different level than eighth graders who are on their way to high school, are responsible for the building blocks of historical skills. Their abilities aren't honed and used in more abstract and global ways until they are in eighth grade. Students may enter sixth grade struggling to read expository text, but (depending on

Table 9.1 Skills Scope and Sequence

Skill	6th Grade	7th Grade	8th Grade
Research	Be able to state the main idea from text.	State the main idea and provide supporting details.	Strong facility in paraphrasing: read and put in your own words what's important.
	Choose and cite quotes from a text.	Choose and cite quotes from a text in MLA format.	Know when and how to cite.
	Compare and contrast different websites on the same topic. Evaluate website extension.	Look at website funders, other articles written by same authors, start looking for language that reveals emotion.	Evaluate Internet source reliability.
	Navigate a table of contents, index, glossary and appendices with guidance.	Navigate a table of contents, index, glossary and appendices with less guidance.	Use a book as a reference tool independently.
	Students can conduct their research based on teacher-provided web resources. Teacher models examples of reliable websites.	Students can use some teacher-provided resources and also supplement with their own findings.	Independently use the Internet for academic purposes.

Skill	6th Grade	7th Grade	8th Grade
Writing	Write a paragraph with a strong topic sentence, three supporting relevant details, and a concluding sentence.	Write an essay based on a two-or-three-pronged thesis statement. Includes body paragraphs that support the thesis, and a conclusion. Completed using teacher-provided scaffolding.	Write a thesis-driven essay that includes body paragraphs that support the thesis and a conclusion by the end of the year with limited to no scaffolding.
Primary/ Secondary Source	Be able to differentiate between a primary and secondary source.	Identify the merits of primary sources and secondary sources.	Should be able to research and find reliable and relevant primary and secondary source documents.
Reading	Use headings and page layout features to assist students in the process of scanning and aiding comprehension of text.	Contextualizing graphs, charts, and sidebars to help discern important information, trends, and to aid in comprehension of text.	Should be able to read and comprehend grade-level, or above, expository text and discern main ideas and important details.
Perspective	Expose to different perspectives of historical events—especially through primary source accounts—and then discuss the reason behind the differing perspectives.	When presented with differing perspectives, students should be able to start identifying them on their own.	Be able to look at multiple perspectives of a historical event and draw conclusion about said historical event/ history in general from differences and similarities.
Geography	Identify cardinal directions. Read a map key. Understand the difference between political and topographical maps. Longitude and latitude.	Examine map changes based on political territorial changes over time.	Look at map projections and determine what bias is present.

whether there are additional factors that may need to be addressed), with scaffolding in reading expository history text, along with work on annotation and reading comprehension strategies, history students can gain increased facility by the end of eighth grade.

How to Measure?

The question then is how to measure each of these skills. Sure, they could be assessed as stand-alone skills, but it's better, of course, that they are seamlessly incorporated with content. This way, when assessing, both the content and the skills are married together. Teachers need to be careful, then, to make sure students feel sufficiently prepared and familiar with the skill being asked of them. They need sufficient scaffolding and practice, since it can be a challenge for them to do two distinct and particularly difficult things at one (use content and apply a new skill). There is also the option of making the content accessible for students to use when being assessed for a particular skill. For example, when I asked students to do timed writing, they were already putting together a myriad of different skills to be able to write a cohesive essay, so I did not require them to memorize content at the same time. They needed to use it but could access it through research and through their notes while writing. To have students *recall* content through memorization when you want to see how well they can *synthesize* content through writing isn't necessarily advantageous for the student—or the teacher. Having too many variables makes it too difficult for us as teachers to be able to see what students know and are able to do.

Many of these skills can also be built and assessed through activities and projects, and don't necessarily need to be tested formally. If students complete a body bio and are able to research and paraphrase and explain what they've found, they don't need to take a test to see if they can research; they've demonstrated it by *doing* it.

And Content?

It can be difficult for those of us who are more focused on the content of history class to see the need for spending precious time developing skills (which can take a good amount of time to scaffold) during the year. But there are several good arguments for working on skills. Students can access historical content in a way they never could before; they can press a button and find out information that I would have had to spend time going to the library and researching. However, the information they find needs to be unpacked— and students need increasingly complex skills in order to be able to unpack and evaluate the information they find. Additionally, these are skills that history classes in high school and college require. There is no reason why we can't begin asking our middle schools students to work at a developmentally appropriate, rigorous level now. English learners, too, can use these skills across disciplines. It may be difficult for them to comprehend the academic language and historical terminology of history class, but with scaffolds in place and with familiar formats and skills, they can work on mastering the skills and find success in that.

> Content doesn't need to be thrown out in favor of skills, but content and skills can be merged seamlessly to create a learning experience that requires students to think *about* content in new ways.

Content doesn't need to be thrown out in favor of skills, but content and skills can be merged seamlessly to create a learning experience that requires students to think *about* content in new ways.

Reflection

One very strong element of assessment that both teachers and students should employ is reflection. For teachers, this can be a process you've trained yourself to do. After a lesson or unit, I write down in an Evernote folder what I need to change or tweak in order to make the lesson better. It's a habit that I have had since my teaching internship program, where there was a real emphasis on teacher reflection. Sometimes though, and especially the first year of teaching, this can feel like a burden when the goal is just to survive the day. However, *any* small amount of habitual reflection that you can (preferably) write down will help make reflection an ingrained habit. And the reflection allows you to break from the trap of "I've always done it this way," as it really requires you to justify each choice that is made and whether it is of the moment, relevant, and most importantly, beneficial for students.

Reflection as Formative Assessment

Students, too, can use reflective processes to see what they understand and what they still need to work on. These reflections can be invaluable formative assessments so that students can readjust and adapt to what they know so far, and what they don't yet understand. KWL (Know, Want to know, Learned) charts can be a good start, but since they are often used in a whole class, students don't always see them as individual mandates to learn something. Instead, you can use prompts in the form of exit cards—either on an actual piece of paper, in an online format such as Lino or Padlet, or on a communal space like an IdeaPaint wall. For example:

1. One thing I really understand from this lesson/unit/etc.
2. One thing I am still not clear on

1. One thing I feel confident about in history class right now
2. Something I am still struggling with

These types of exit questions can go a long way in getting students in the habit of thinking metacognitively about their own thinking. *Do* they understand what is happening? Many middle school students will blissfully go through their days not thinking about whether they understand *anything* they learn. This isn't a negative thing so much as a developmental part of being of middle school age. Students still might have a stronger sense of their abilities than is realistic—or they might not be conscious enough yet to even *think* about it. They might only think about it once they've already received an end-of-term grade. Asking them, making them reach to think about whether they are understanding, whether they are doing it naturally or not, will get them into the habit of doing so. Not to mention the fact that the data collected from reflective formative assessments is helpful for the teacher to be able to see what students understand. This reflective cycle, where the teacher has students reflect on their understanding, gathers the data, and reads it carefully to then reflect on his or her own teaching, can only be beneficial for these students in the long run.

Summative Assessments

Although formative assessments are invaluable, when people think about assessments, they typically think of summative assessments—tests, projects, or activities at the end of a unit that show what a student has learned from said unit. Summative information can be very valuable to teachers as they reflect on how a unit went and what changes might be in order. But the information really won't benefit current students unless there's a pressing need to reteach material or skills. On the other hand, summative assessments *can* do more than just give information and data to the teacher and the student. They can also be a way for students to feel ownership of the skills and content they've been studying, and a way to show an audience what they know and are able to do.

Tests, Projects, Rubrics, and Essays

If summative assessments are what people think of when they think of the word "assessment," the most common summative assessment people think of are tests. Tests have changed over time. While there are still plenty of multiple-choice tests in use, they don't usually measure much other than memorization, content, and the student's ability to take a multiple-choice test. They aren't useless, but they aren't necessarily the *best* way to see if a student understands material. They're often something that students "cram" for. Cramming and memorization often result in a brain dump the day of the test, and the material, stored in short-term memory, can be lost forever (Glenn, 2007). Teachers are sometimes baffled that their students don't remember details that they know they taught the previous year—or even of the previous unit—but often this relationship between storing knowledge in short-term memory and then regurgitating it for a test is to blame.

Personally, I like to use tests that require students to apply the content and skills that have been learned. For example, for a test on the Bill of Rights, I ask students to read through a scenario in which a person's rights are violated in multiple ways. Students need to read the scenario closely and then explain which rights should have been protected based on those protected by the Bill of Rights. The students are still required to know the Bill of Rights—the number and the rights it protects—but they aren't just filling in blanks. They have to apply the Bill of Rights to an actual scenario.

Projects, as discussed in Chapter 8, can also be an important way to gauge student understanding. They provide an authentic way for students to share their understandings with their peers. The learning from these kinds of projects are much more likely to be stored in long-term memory, rather than in short-term memory, where it would be dumped out at first notice. Projects do need to be graded, though (if you teach in a grade-based school), and this can be a challenge, especially if students are submitting different kinds of projects. Some will aver that project-based learning assignments should be graded as "credit/no credit"—either the student completes the project according to expectations that can be pre-delineated or they do not. Some teachers want a more categorical breakdown of what students were able to demonstrate in terms of knowledge, skills, creativity, and presentation. In these cases, each skill and or content area should be broken up into categories and then gauged on a rubric. This way, students will be able to see what parts of their project or essay needed improvement.

Essays (spoken about more in Chapter 5) can also be graded with a rubric so students can see which skills they need to spend more time on, and which they have mastered.

Students can even have a hand in creating the rubrics; this will give them ownership of the level of quality that they are expected to produce for a given piece of writing or a project.

These rubrics can help students better their writing and not just see writing as something that they turn in once and are done with. Collaborating in Google Drive can serve a similar purpose. If the student, another peer, and the teacher engage in the process of peer editing on Google Drive together, the student is then pushed to go through multiple revisions in order to reach expectations. This process of revision can become normative and habitual, breaking students from the cycle of turning in their first drafts which are often (and why not?) riddled with errors. Reflecting, reiterating, and revising helps students see the inherent learning in the assessment process. After all, all the effort can't just be for a grade.

> Reflecting, reiterating, and revising helps students see the inherent learning in the assessment process. After all, all the effort can't just be for a grade.

Presentations

Students often give presentations as part of class—especially when projects are involved. However, students often need to be coached on presentation strategies; they can't just "wing it." We should teach public speaking skills, eye contact, how to arrange the content of slides, what to say, and what to show, etc. Without guidance, students will often just get up and read off their slideshow, which can be painful for the presenters to engage in and painful for the audience to listen to. Students can practice presentation skills throughout the year. We can model presentation skills explicitly (not just embed them into a lesson), and students can build together, as a class, a presentation that is concise and interesting to listen to. Students can take turns reading in a loud, clear voice and making eye contact with the audience. Practice and discussion of what *makes* a good presentation (and for what context and audience) can be invaluable for students. And once they've worked on these skills, *then* presentation skills can be assessed on a rubric or as part of a presentation. And with technology, these presentations and projects can be presented to a larger audience, whether to younger grades, the school as a whole, or even to the world beyond.

Standardized Tests

Despite the many alternate modes of summative assessment that are out there, many teachers are beholden to high-stakes standardized testing, or, perhaps to regular-stakes standardized testing. The reality is that most of us teachers need to give standardized tests to their history students at one time or another. And this is a challenge. Best practices in education don't always align with what is being measured on a standardized test. Often students are asked about specific content on these tests, and so teachers are forced to cover particular content, drill it, and have students memorize it so that students can then can achieve a good score. This of course, runs into the issue of whether the students would be able to perform on the same standardized test later in the year or the following year—likely not, due to the cramming and short-term memory issues discussed earlier.

However, some tests are better than others. Tests where students are given primary/secondary sources to analyze and then write about, for example, are usually better than multiple choice because students can use historical *skills* to show what they know. Students are being tested then on their skill of synthesizing and writing about text they've read in the moment. And content isn't lost in this format; if students are given primary or secondary source documents about the Byzantine Empire, they will likely need some context and background information in their brain in order to piece together a coherent, cogent, and well-argued response.

While I can appreciate the pressure from administration, districts, and even parents that is being placed on teachers to raise history standardized test scores, I would argue that teachers still need to teach "like nobody's watching." Based on research about content cramming, it isn't advantageous in the long term to prepare students for standardized tests only so that they can pass them. It is much better to teach history in a meaningful way, to engage, to reflect, to work on lasting historical skills, in order to make important connections. If the preparation for standardized tests is embedded in meaningful learning activities, instead of in cram sessions, it is better for students. Yes, it is important for students to do well on standardized tests because of all of the money, clout, etc. that are attached to them, but it is more important to develop students' skills and instill in them a love of learning history so that they can be successful in the subject and *want* to continue learning. If they burn out and don't care about history because they've been drilled and killed to death, the magic will go out of the subject, and they won't want to study it ever again. That can't be what we want.

Intangibles

Standardized tests are, well, standardized. They might give some tangible evidence of whatever is being assessed, but how do you assess for the intangibles? Are students ready for high school? Do they *like* history? These things, though harder to measure, are important. But how do we measure them? You can do this by checking engagement (whether students work in class), by doing both self and student reflections, and by checking if students feel like they are able to do the work, but are still challenged in class. These intangibles and measures that are difficult to assess may not be the information that states and administrations need to demonstrate success, but they can be buoys for you, the teacher, to know that you are helping students to connect to their world and to the past in a way that is meaningful to them.

How Has Assessment Changed?

When I was in middle school, the expectations seemed a little looser. These days, as a result of No Child Left Behind and other factors, middle school students have to meet increased state and national standards that they are then beholden to on standardized tests. Essays seem to have gotten harder, too. But students also have opportunities to express what they know in other ways, such as through project-based learning. The most important thing to remember is that middle schoolers are different from elementary and high school students. They need to be engaged differently, so it follows they need to show what they know differently. Students need varied assessments; they need to be able to show what they know in multiple ways, to be able to access different skills and talents, and to be able to demonstrate understanding. And

> Students need varied assessments; they need to be able to show what they know in multiple ways, to be able to access different skills and talents, and to be able to demonstrate understanding.

we, as their teachers, need assessment to be able to continue to reflect, change, and progress in order to meet the needs of our students.

Chapter 9 Self-Reflection

1. Do you use student assessment as a tool for self-reflection? How?
2. How do you use student self-reflection in your classroom?
3. To what extent do standards dictate assessment in your classroom? How does that affect your teaching?
4. What strategies from this chapter are you thinking of utilizing?
5. What adjustments might you need to make for your own classroom and the needs of your students?

References

Glenn, David. "Why Cramming Doesn't Work." *Chronicle of Higher Education* 53.40 (2007): A17. *ERIC*. Web. 13 Sep. 2015.

Walker, Karen, Principals' Partnership, and Foundation Union Pacific. "Optimal Testing Environment. Research Brief." *Principals' Partnership* (2010): *ERIC*. Web. 10 Sep. 2015.

10

Epilogue

What Is the Future of History in Middle School?

When Shara Peters, Aaron Brock, and I were thinking of names for our social studies blog for MiddleWeb, we came up with *Future of History*. Yes, we were trying to be clever—future, history . . . get it? But really the meaning is much larger. History as a subject is here to stay, but how we teach history and how students go about learning history is very much open for discussion.

Why all this discussion *now*? The advent of technology has made a few important changes to the study of history in schools. One, it has made it much easier for teachers to interact about pedagogy, technological tools, and content in order to learn more and share more about the practice. But even more, it has fundamentally changed the way students learn about history. In the past, books and teachers were the holders of historical facts and information. Historical analysis was saved for college, and students needed a broad range of specific historical information in order to be literate human beings in society. These facts that students worked so hard to contextualize and memorize came more easily to some, harder to others. Students did occasionally get to engage in fun activities, but the activities were ancillary to the main goals: learn the information, keep the information.

A New History Teacher

History teachers still need to know a lot about content. But now they aren't the only ones who know the content. In the past, that was the value of the history teacher, the person who knew *everything*—or at least knew where to look. Today, history teachers don't have to have that kind of clout, because they certainly aren't alone as the holders of all of the information about history and historical analysis. Why, my students can look up the information on the Internet. They might not be able to understand all of it or discern the most important parts, but helping them with that part is my job. Telling them that the Battle of Bunker Hill really should have been called the Battle of Breed's Hill—that is no longer privileged information.

So then who are we now as history teachers? It may be that we are going through a bit of an identity crisis as a result of all of these changes. And this affects our students, too. In middle school, they are going through their own identity crisis, and they need us to be able to make it through ours in order to help them with theirs.

Pedagogy Whiplash in the Age of the Internet

We want to prepare our middle school history students for the world that *they* will inhabit in their own futures, not prepare them for the world from our pasts. This, I think most educators would agree with. What we don't all agree with is exactly *how* to accomplish this. While John Dewey's principles of learning through experiencing (1964) aren't new at all, there *are* new schools of thought popping up daily on exactly how students can learn by doing in the technological age. Proponents of the Maker Movement, project-based learning, and other new kinds of pedagogies aver that learning by doing, making, and creating is the highest form of education. They say that *this* will be the way to prepare our students for the future. Conversely, the messages many are receiving from state and federal governments are that more coverage is necessary, and the development of basic skills is the only

> We want to prepare our middle school history students for the world that *they* will inhabit in their own futures, not prepare them for the world from our pasts.

way to prepare students for their futures as productive U.S. citizens. Some educators extol the virtues of covering content and feel that giving students a comprehensive and contextualized understanding of historical content, and its effects on the present, is the correct way to teach history today. So what is right? And how on earth is a teacher to know? The downside to the technological revolution is that so much is being shared, it is difficult to know what to believe and what is right. I have a hard time believing that one way is best for education. I have to imagine that as people are complex, so is the road to learning. The road may be overgrown with brush at times, and difficult to pass, but ultimately it will lead to somewhere interesting where we've never been. That has to be the goal, and there can't just be one way to get there. As teachers, we have to pick and choose the types of pedagogical strategies that we think, and that our team and administration agree, will be best for the unique needs of our students.

> As teachers, we have to pick and choose the types of pedagogical strategies that we think, and that our team and administration agree, will be best for the unique needs of our students.

The most important thing, though, is to *question and to seek* what is best for our students, despite the pedagogical whiplash that can occur as a result of the search. I am not advocating for us to give up the quest because the cacophony of voices is too loud and discordant. Rather, we can adopt a quiet, measured, and reflective approach to introducing new pedagogy; this can be much more effective than introducing each and every new thing that you encounter. And this can be *much* more effective than *not* seeking out new ways of learning and teaching students, opting simply for doing what is easiest, what has been done in the past.

Rallying the Support of the Community

It is advantageous to remember though, that with this challenge of increased vocality on the Internet about what is best and what is right, there is also the benefit of having so many resources to tap into in order to be able to answer our questions and in order to learn new things. We can follow historians on Twitter to learn more about content and what the current thoughts are on a particular topic, as well as follow distinguished educators and educational luminaries who are blogging and discussing what works for them in the classroom. Twitter and other like communities (see Appendix A) are an amazing resource for teachers of all disciplines, history or otherwise, and if you aren't part of the conversation yet, I can't suggest any more strongly that you join us.

The Liminality of the Middle School Student Experience, the Liminality of the History Educator's Experience

So if it isn't completely clear as to what exactly the right thing to do is in order to educate our students for the future, then how can we, well, teach? It can be a challenge to look beyond the way one has been taught, beyond how we may have learned how to teach in our teacher preparation programs. We may need to try, iterate, fail, reflect, and try again in order to see what can work for our students—just as we ask them to do, too.

As you saw in this book, I take a varied approach in my teaching. I value student-centered learning, skill building, autonomy, and learning for the sake of learning very highly, but I also know that middle school students require certain structural elements in order to be successful. It is a balancing act—we as middle school teachers need to be flexible, varied, but structured, and ultimately we need to be risk-takers. Middle school history students are at a crossroads themselves; their liminal stage is less of a revolutionary situation and more an age-old liminal stage of development. But it is wise for us middle school history teachers to reflect on how our current state of pedagogical liminality may reflect the very state of the middle schoolers we teach. Where are we going? Who are we? How will be make our own path and give back to others? What makes our progression unique? How will we distinguish ourselves, yet align ourselves with other disciplines?

> It is a balancing act—we as middle school teachers need to be flexible, varied, but structured, and ultimately we need to be risk-takers.

Who Should We Be? How Should We Teach?

Being in a liminal stage in education—a crossroads, an evolutionary moment—can be a challenge, but it is more of an opportunity than a difficulty. As mentioned earlier, one important way to be present is to listen to other voices and to gather and be open to as many ideas about teaching history and teaching middle schoolers, and just plain *teaching*, as possible.

But the other part is to be reflective, and that reflection can be done privately or publicly. Privately, a teacher can try new things, try out new pedagogies, look at history content in a new way, and make changes to his or her student's learning experiences based on research and trial and error. But why not share these experiences? It can be difficult opening up a classroom in this way; for so long, teaching was quite an isolated business. But that is part of this evolution. Being transparent, being open about our practice is a benefit of being educators at this moment. You may feel vulnerable or worry that what you have to share isn't unique or worthy, but I can tell you that, to someone, it will be helpful. There is rarely a book for educators where each and every piece of advice or information is novel in and of itself, but there is always a gem of importance that will stand out for you; something you can take back to the classroom. So why not be the creator and disseminator of those gems of teaching history yourself? We need to share our voices in order to help each other through this liminal stage, to grow together and share together.

Technology

I purposefully didn't devote a particular section or chapter in this book to discuss technology in a vacuum because, at this point, technology permeates educational culture—either through its abundance or through its marked lack. I strongly believe that to progress as educators, we need to embrace technology in classrooms for what it can offer our students and their learning experiences. Are there pitfalls and challenges? For sure. Can we better prepare our students by guiding them through these challenges rather than avoiding them? Absolutely. There is also the question of technology use for technology's sake rather than purposeful technology use. It goes without saying that I advocate for the purposeful use of technology in the classroom á la the SAMR (Substitution, Augmentation, Modification, and Redefinition) model, in which technology isn't used simply as a fancy replacement for what we were doing already, but instead provides students with ways to innovate and create something that they weren't capable of doing without the technology.

And then there is the issue of access. There are still many schools in the United States that, due to socioeconomic and political factors, are without access to the Internet and basic technology. In this day and age and in public schools, this is unconscionable. There are ways to adapt twenty-first century learning and skills without technology, but it puts such a burden on the teacher and keeps students away from the learning of the world. This is a separate issue but one that is incredibly important and needs to be addressed.

Figure 10.1 SAMR Model

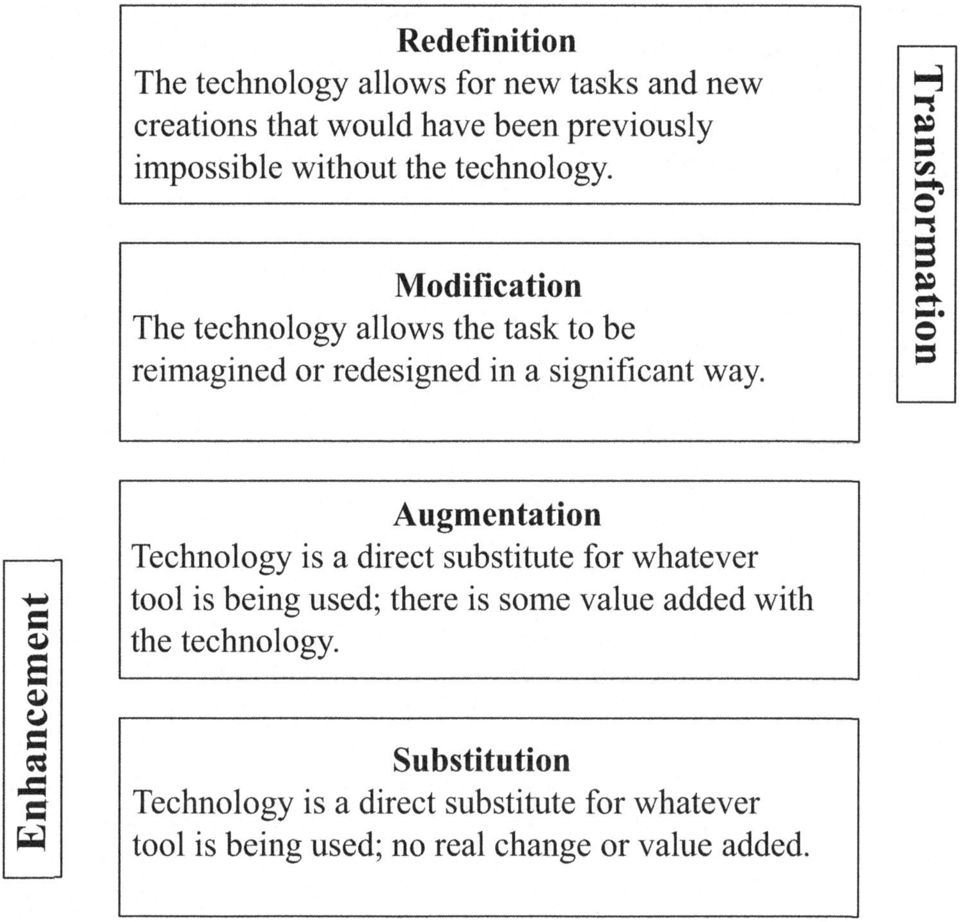

Redefinition The technology allows for new tasks and new creations that would have been previously impossible without the technology.	**Transformation**
Modification The technology allows the task to be reimagined or redesigned in a significant way.	
Augmentation Technology is a direct substitute for whatever tool is being used; there is some value added with the technology.	
Substitution Technology is a direct substitute for whatever tool is being used; no real change or value added.	**Enhancement**

Students' Technology Use

And it might be that as teachers we feel our students know more than we do about technology, so to incorporate it is redundant. Or we might feel that students get enough technology in their homes, so they need a place to learn free of digital distractions. The question here isn't about use or disuse, but rather quality of use. Teachers, regardless of whether they are in Marc Prensky's (2001) class of digital natives or digital immigrants, are immensely important to students to be able to help them navigate the digital world. Students may be able to use the technology, but it doesn't mean they are using it ethically, consciously, or purposefully. They might know how to watch people playing video games on YouTube, or be able to access the latest meme via Tumblr, but they may not know how to find out information that will be increasingly important for them to learn and know as time goes on. They need help being able to look for results beyond the first thing that pops up in a Google search, they need help learning how to press pause before a status update, they need help from their teachers and community in disengaging from social media and technology when things get overwhelming, and they need help figuring out what information is useful and what is unreliable. The list goes on. So students are navigating these new seas of technology as well. Just because they have been using technology all their lives, doesn't mean they are adept. Guiding them is our job; history class is an important place to seamlessly blend in these technology skills with the content and historiography we want to focus on. We can't underestimate students' abilities, but we can't leave them hanging for support and guidance either. They are middle schoolers.

Standards

So it isn't surprising then, with all this educational tumult, that standards have adjusted to address these changes and education is adjusting to address the standards. In my practice, I am guided by California State Standards and the Common Core Standards for history http://www.corestandards.org/ELA-Literacy/RH/6-8/. As mentioned in Chapter 1, these standards emphasize not the content of history, but the skills of close reading, critical thinking, and discerning of bias in primary and secondary sources. These skills are piggybacking on the natural changes in the history classroom, where the content is embedded into the experience and application of these skills, rather than the other way around. Remember, these standards can be achieved through multiple pedagogical approaches—there isn't one way to get students to think. We can continue innovating and coming up with new ideas to connect students to history and make it relevant to their lives now.

Students now have to think more critically than students in my day. Instead of just knowing things, they have to really work to analyze history. And this makes sense, because they are encountering much more text and media than ever before.

What Is the Future of Teaching and Learning in Middle School?

Middle school is a time for learning how a person can fit into a time and place. Students are figuring out how to navigate the world socially, emotionally, and, occasionally, academically. They are both idealistic and self-centered—they are angered at injustice and they mete out injustices. They are open to learning and have the skills to learn, but they are also distracted and distractible. History is about people, about culture. We need to make sure that whatever content is being taught, whatever pedagogy is being used, that the study of history is made relevant to students, and that somehow it touches their lives. Whether we have students study their own culture and see themselves in history in a new way through alternatives to the dominant narrative, or whether we show them how the past has affected the present, or whether we inspire them to act in the world—we need to make it about them, the students. We must study students to figure out what they need. They are part of history, too. Teach them *that*.

> We must study students to figure out what they need. They are part of history, too. Teach them *that*.

References

Dewey, John, and Reginald D. Archambault. *John Dewey on Education: Selected Writings*. New York: Modern Library, 1964. Print.

"History/Social Studies: Grade 6–8." English Language Arts Standards. N.p., n.d. Web. 13 Sep. 2015.

Prensky, Marc. "Digital Natives, Digital Immigrants." *On the Horizon* 9.5 (2001): N.p. MCB University Press. Web. 13 Sep. 2015. <http://www.marcprensky.com/writing/Prensky%20-%20Digital%20Natives,%20Digital%20Immigrants%20-%20Part1.pdf>.

"SAMR." *Kathy Schrock's Guide to Everything*. N.p., n.d. Web. 13 Sep. 2015.

Appendix A
Resources from Each Chapter

Chapter 1: Introduction: Teaching Middle School History: It's Not Quite Elementary School . . . It's Not Quite High School

Brain Research about Teenagers/Middle Schoolers

◆ Giedd, Jay N. "Risky Teen Behavior Is Driven by an Imbalance in Brain Development." *Scientific American Global RSS*. N.p., June 2015. Web. 27 July 2015. <http://www.scientificamerican.com/article/risky-teen-behavior-is-driven-by-an-imbalance-in-brain-development/>.

Chapter 2: Day to Day: Providing Structure and Routines for a Middle School History Classroom

Collaborative Tools

◆ IdeaPaint: a tool that turns a wall into a white board <https://www.ideapaint.com>.

◆ Padlet: an online collaborative tool which allows students to post responses online all at the same time <https://padlet.com>.

◆ Lino Board: another online collaborative tool which allows students to post information and ideas on a virtual Post-It <http://en.linoit.com>.

Articles and Books for Reference

◆ Passanisi, Jody. "Confronting My Flipped Classroom Bias." *MiddleWeb*. N.p., 29 Dec. 2013. Web. 30 Sep. 2015. <http://www.middleweb.com/11419/confronting-flipped-classroom-bias/>.

◆ Gnaulati, Enrico. *Back to Normal: Why Ordinary Childhood Behavior Is Mistaken for ADHD, Bipolar Disorder, and Autism Spectrum Disorder*. Boston: Beacon, 2013. E-book.

◆ May, Cindi. "A Learning Secret: Don't Take Notes with a Laptop." *Scientific American Global RSS*. N.p., 3 June 2014. Web. 11 Aug. 2015. <http://www.scientificamerican.com/article/a-learning-secret-don-t-take-notes-with-a-laptop/>.

Chapter 3: Comprehension and Analysis of Expository Texts in History: What Does It Say? What Does It Mean?

Articles and Books for Reference from this Chapter

◆ Social Studies School Service: www.socialstudies.com
◆ Heafner, Tina, and Dixie Massey. *Strategic Reading in U.S. History.* Culver City, CA: Social Studies School Service, 2006. Print.
◆ Raphael, T.E. "Teaching Question-Answer Relationships." *The Reading Teacher*, 39 (1986): 516–520.

Chapter 4: Evaluation of Text: What's the Perspective?

Articles and Books for Reference from this Chapter

◆ Stanford History Education Group (SHEG): sheg.stanford.edu
◆ Common Sense Media: https://www.commonsensemedia.org

Chapter 5: Writing in History: Making Arguments, Backing Them Up, and Citing Sources

Links to Student Blog Hosting Sites

◆ Edublogs: https://edublogs.org
◆ Kidblog: https://kidblog.org

Chapter 6: Relevance: Why Does This Matter To Me? Social Context, Historical Legacy, and Current Events

Articles and Sites Referenced in this Chapter

◆ Mr. Betts's parody: "What Does John Locke Say?" https://www.youtube.com/watch?v=kItXvJLnTtk
◆ Ta-Nehisi Coates's article "The Case for Reparations" http://www.theatlantic.com/magazine/archive/2014/06/the-case-for-reparations/361631/
◆ The USC Shoah Foundation: http://sfi.usc.edu
◆ Facing History and Ourselves: https://www.facinghistory.org

Chapter 7: Engagement: Historical Figures, Field Trips, and Games

Selection of Sites with Virtual Field Trips

- ◆ National Museum of Natural History: http://www.mnh.si.edu/vtp/1-desktop/
- ◆ Scholastic's Virtual Tour of Ellis Island: http://teacher.scholastic.com/activities/immigration/tour/
- ◆ The Louvre: http://www.louvre.fr/en/visites-en-ligne
- ◆ Mt. Vernon: http://www.mountvernon.org/site/virtual-tour
- ◆ Colonial Williamsburg: http://tour.history.org
- ◆ Gettysburg: http://www.virtualgettysburg.com
- ◆ The U.S. Capitol: http://www.capitol.gov/#THMESEC_20100 61447464 I THME_2010062211742
- ◆ The White House: https://www.whitehouse.gov/about/inside-white-house/interactive-tour
- ◆ China's Forbidden City: http://www.thechinaguide.com/index.php?action=activity/view&activity_id=2
- ◆ The Great Wall of China: http://www.thechinaguide.com/index.php?action=activity/greatWallOfChina
- ◆ Historic center of Urbino: http://whc.unesco.org/en/list/828/gallery/

Chapter 8: Inquiry: Project-Based Learning

Articles and Books for Reference from this Chapter

- ◆ Berger, Ron. *An Ethic of Excellence: Building a Culture of Craftsmanship with Students.* Portsmouth, NH: Heinemann, 2003. Print.
- ◆ Dweck, Carol S. *Mindset: The New Psychology of Success.* New York: Random House, 2006. Print.
- ◆ Buck Institute of Education: http://bie.org

Chapter 10: Epilogue: What Is the Future of History in Middle School?

Connecting with Social Media

- ◆ Twitter Hashtags for Educators and Social Studies Teachers: www.twitter.com #historyteacher, #sschat, #edchat

Articles and Books for Reference from this Chapter

- ◆ Dewey, John, and Reginald D. Archambault. *John Dewey on Education: Selected Writings*. New York: Modern Library, 1964. Print.
- ◆ "History/Social Studies: Grade 6–8." English Language Arts Standards. N.p., n.d. Web. 13 Sep. 2015.
- ◆ "SAMR." *Kathy Schrock's Guide to Everything*. N.p., n.d. Web. 13 Sep. 2015.

Appendix B
Blackline Masters

Notes Protocol

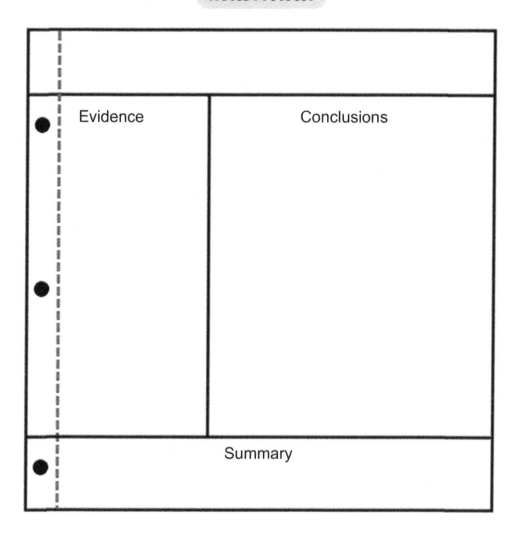

Evidence

Conclusions

Summary

Using Visual Imagery to Help with Textual Understanding

Visual Image	Words and Phrases	Check your Image. Was it correct?

QAR (Question Answer Relationship) Chart

Level 1: Right There: The answer to this question will be in the text in one place and could likely be quoted verbatim.

Level 2: Think and Search: The answer to this question will be in the text, but in a couple different places.

Level 3: The Author and You: The answer is not directly in the text. The student must use the text and his or her own knowledge to answer the question.

Level 4: On Your Own: The answer is not in the text. The text got you thinking and now you must use themes from the text and your own knowledge to construct an answer.

Annotation Strategy

Reading Notes Instructions

1. Set up Notes (this is with the usual notes format discussed in Chapter 2)
2. Use the current Unit and the title of the text you just annotated as the title of the notes
3. Put your first main idea on the left side of the notes
4. Summarize everything you underlined about that main idea on the right side of the notes
5. Repeat steps 3 and 4 with each of your main ideas
6. Write an objective summary at the end of the notes
7. **The objective summary must include all 5 Ws**

Annotation Instructions*:

1. Look for **FOUR** main ideas that will eventually go into your notes
2. Each main idea must be one of the 5 Ws

   a. **Who**: names, groups of people
   b. **When**: years, time periods
   c. **Where**: places, regions
   d. **What**: events, ideas
   e. **Why**: causes, motivations

3. Underline every sentence where you find your main ideas
4. In the margin, label each underlined sentence with the name of the main idea

*Used with permission from Aaron Brock

Inquiry Chart

Topic: **Shays' Rebellion**	Reasons for Rebellion	People involved	Reactions from Government	Results	Other differences
Source 1: Howard Zinn: *Farmers in Revolt*					
Source 2: Excerpt from Paul Johnson's *A History of the American People*					

Conclusions: What were some major differences that you found? What do you think the reasons were for these differences? What does this tell you about Shays' Rebellion?

Different Views of America Chart

Different Views of America   Notes 1

Does Tupac have a positive or negative view of America?

Answer	Evidence

Conclusion

Write a short conclusion, restating Tupac's opinion of America.
Why do you think he feels this way?

Simple Body Bio

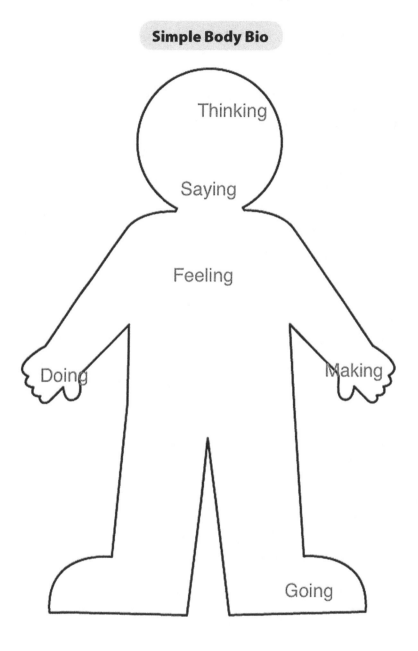

Thinking

Saying

Feeling

Doing

Making

Going

Complex Body Bio

What ideas, people, events, experiences influenced this person? (Make sure they are relevant to the topic.) Include at least three.

What did this person think about the topic? What did this person believe about the world? Include political ideas.

What were some positive things this person did? What positive events may have happened to him/her?

What were some negative things this person did? What bad things may have happened to him/her?

What is in this person's heart? What is truly important to them? What are his/her feelings?